Crockpot Recipes

101 Low Sugar Slow Cooker Recipes

©Copyright Recipe Junkies

Paleo Crock Pot Chicken and Kale Soup

Serves: 8

Preparation Time: 6 hours 45 minutes

Ingredients

- Chicken thighs (2 lbs, skinless)

- Garlic (2 cloves, minced)

- Thyme (2 sprigs, fresh)

- Chicken broth (5 cups)

- Yellow Onion (1, chopped)

- Carrots (1 lb, sliced lengthwise)

- Kale (4 cups, chopped)

- Pepper

Directions

1. Put chicken into crock pot and add garlic and thyme on top.

2. Pour broth into pot and set on high.

3. Cook for 4 hours until meat is tender and falls off the bone. Take chicken from pot and put into a container. Take thyme from pot and throw away.

4. Strain broth into a container then return to pot.

5. Remove bones from chicken and shred the chicken gently. Put the bones back into soup and set on high.

6. Put shredded chicken into refrigerator.

7. Add onion, pepper and carrots and cook for 90 minutes. Remove bones from soup and taste.

8. Add kale to soup and cook for an additional 30 minutes. Then add shredded chicken to soup, cook for 10 minutes and serve.

Nutritional Information

- Calories 172

- Fat 4.03g

- Saturated Fat 1.21 g

- Carbohydrates 8.3 g

- Sugar 1.7 g

- Protein 23.4 g

- Cholesterol 106. 5 g

Paleo Fresh Summer Crock Pot Lasagna

Serves: 6

Preparation Time: 2 hours 30 minutes

Ingredients

Marinara:

- Olive oil (1/4 cup)

- Onion (1, diced)

- Garlic (1 teaspoon., diced)

- Honey (1/2 tablespoon)

- Tomatoes (7 cups, diced)

Meat Filling:

- Olive oil (1 tablespoon)

- Onion (1/2, chopped)

- Ground turkey (1 lb)

- Basil leaves (1 cup, chopped)

- Pepper

Paleo 'Cheese Sauce'

- Onion (1/2, chopped)

- Olive Oil (1/2 teaspoon)

- Yellow summer squash (1/2, diced)

- Coconut Milk (1/2 cup)

- Vegan Cheddar (1/2cup)

- Zucchini (4, sliced thinly lengthwise)

Directions

1. *Make marinara-* Use a large saucepan to heat oil over a medium flame, put in onions and sauté for 2 minutes. Add garlic and cook for 1 minute. Put in honey and tomatoes and lower flame and cook for 20 minutes until it starts to thicken.

2. *Make meat filling-* Use a large skillet to heat oil and cook onion, pepper and turkey for 2 minutes using a spoon to break it up. Cook until onion is soft. Take pan from flame and add basil and toss.

3. *Make 'cheese sauce'-* Use a small saucepan to heat oil. Add squash, garlic and onion and cook for 4 minutes. Then put in ¼ cup coconut milk and boil for 2 minutes till liquid has reduced. Then put in cheese and stir. Put sauce into blender along with leftover coconut milk and blend till smooth.

4. *Put lasagna together-*Oil the bottom of your crock pot and spread ¾ cup of marinara in it. Arrange 5 slices of zucchini laid beside one another and spoon about ½ cup of cheese sauce on top of that. Then add ½ cup of meat on top of sauce and top with another ½ cup of sauce.

5. Repeat until 5 layers have been made. Top with marinara.

6. Set pot on high and cover. Cook for 1 ½ hours.

7. Remove excess liquid from the pot by using a turkey baster.

8. Put sauce into a sauce pan and boil till thickened then put on top of lasagna and serve.

Nutritional Information

- Calories 198

- Fat 12.3 g

- Saturated Fat 4.8 g

- Carbohydrates 8 g

- Sugar 4.9 g

- Protein 13.5 g

- Cholesterol 68 g

Paleo Crockpot Cauliflower Rice

Serves: 4

Preparation Time: 3 hours 30 minutes

Ingredients

- Cauliflower (2 heads)

- Garlic (1 tablespoon)

- Ginger (1 tablespoon)

- Vegetable broth (1/2 cup)

- Green Peas (1/4 cup)

- Frozen/canned Corn (1/2 cup)

- Scallions (1/4 cup)

Directions

1. Cut florets from cauliflower and crush using a food processor.

2. Put crumbled cauliflower into crock pot along with broth, ginger and garlic.

3. Set crock pot on low and cook for 3 hours.

4. Add corn, cilantro and scallion and toss. Cook for 30 minutes.

Nutritional Information (for chicken)

- Calories 86

- Fat 5 g

- Saturated Fat 2 g

- Carbohydrates 22 g

- Sugar 6 g

- Protein 13 g

- Cholesterol 82g

Paleo Crockpot Chicken Tikka Masala

Serves: 6

Preparation Time: 4 hours

Ingredients

- Chicken breasts (2 ¼ cups, skinned and cubed)

- Yellow Onion (1/2, minced)

- Ginger (2 tablespoons, grated finely)

- Garlic (4 cloves, minced)

- Cashew crème (1 cup)- recipe included below

- Tomato puree (1/2 cup)

- Almond milk (1 ½ cups)

- Olive oil (2 tablespoons)

- Garam Masala (2 tablespoons)

- Lemon Juice (2 tablespoons)

- Ground cumin (1/2 tablespoon)

- Celtic salt (2 teaspoons)

- Bay leaves (2)

- Cayenne pepper (2 teaspoons)

- Arrowroot powder (1 tablespoon)

- Red Pepper (1, de-seeded, halved)

- Cilantro (chopped)

- Cauliflower rice

Directions

1. Make cashew crème- Put 1 cup of cashews in 3 cups of hot water for half an hour. Drain water from cashew and put water aside till needed. Using a blender, cream cashews using 1 cup of water. Add more water if mixture is too thick.

2. Use a large bowl to combine, garlic, tomato puree, ½ cup milk, onions, ginger, cashew crème, lemon juice, paprika, cinnamon, cayenne pepper, olive oil, garam masala and pepper.

3. Stir mixture together and put half of mixture into a crock pot. Put in chicken and top with leftover sauce.

4. Put in bay leaves and red pepper.

5. Set Crockpot on high and cook for 3 hours.

6. Whip together arrowroot and leftover milk. Pour mixture into Crockpot and cook for 20 minutes.

7. Serve over cauliflower rice.

Nutritional Information (for chicken)

- Calories 450

- Fat 13.3 g

- Carbohydrates 12 g

Paleo Crockpot White Bean Chili

Serves: 4-6

Preparation Time: 4-6 hours

Ingredients

- White beans (4 cups, soaked overnight)

- Vegetable broth (4 cups)

- Tofu (2 cups, cubed)

- Bell pepper (1, diced)

- Yellow onion (1, chopped)

- Garlic (5 cloves, diced)

- Jalapeno (1, diced and seeded)

- Ground cumin (1 tablespoon)

- Paprika- smoked (1 teaspoon)

- Chili powder (1 teaspoon)

- Pepper

- Dried herbs

Directions

1. Rinse and drain beans and add them to a crock pot.

2. Put in all other ingredients and set on low. Stir mixture and cover.

3. Cook for 4-6 hours. Stir in desired amount of dried herbs.

4. Serve and enjoy.

Nutritional Information

- Calories 470

- Fat 6.3 g

- Saturated Fat 1 g

- Carbohydrates 53 g

- Sugar 3.9 g

- Protein 48 g

- Cholesterol 90 g

Mexican Chicken Soup With Cheddar Cheese Chips

Serves: 4-6

Preparation Time: 4-5 hours

Ingredients

- Chicken broth (6 cups)

- Yellow Onion (1/2, chopped)

- Garlic (4 cloves, sliced)

- Tomato juice (1 cup)

- Coriander (1 teaspoon)

- Whole chicken (1, skinned)

- Cilantro (1/2 cup)

- Carrots (3, sliced)

- Poblano pepper (1, seeds removed, diced)

- Tomatoes (3, chopped)

- Lime juice- freshly squeezed

For topping:

- Black beans

- Sour cream

- Cheddar cheese chips (recipe below)

- Avocado

Directions

Make soup:

1. Put ingredients for soup into your crock pot not including cilantro and lime juice. Set crock-pot on high, cover and cook for 3 hours.

2. Take chicken out of pot and shred with a fork. Dispose of bones and put the chicken back into the pot.

3. Put in cilantro and lime juice.

4. Cook for an hour more. Keep warm, serve and enjoy!

Make Cheddar:

1. Use a tablespoon to make mounds of cheese on a lined baking sheet. Bake for 5 minutes at 400°F and remove from oven. Cool, add to soup and enjoy!

Nutritional Information

- Calories 280

- Fat 6.3 g

- Saturated Fat 1 g

- Carbohydrates 12.5 g

- Sugar 4.9 g

- Protein 42.5 g

Enchilada Stuffed Peppers With Chile Verde Sauce

Serves: 4-6

Preparation Time: 1 hour 5 minutes

Ingredients

Sauce:

- Serrano Chilies (2)

- Garlic (3 cloves)

- Tomatillos (1 ½ lbs, rinsed and husked)

- Yellow Onion (1/4)

- Dried herbs (3/4 teaspoon)

Peppers:

- Chicken (1 ½ lbs)

- Yellow onion (1/2 cup, chopped)

- Baby spinach (2 cups)

- Cumin (2 teaspoons)

- Ground Coriander (1 ½ teaspoon)

- Poblano peppers (4-6 large)

- (1 ½ cups, diced)

- Carrots (1 cup, shredded)

- Dried herbs(2 ½ teaspoons)

- Chili powder (1 ½ teaspoons)

- Avocado (topping)

Directions

1. Use a large pot of water to boil and put serrano pepper and tomatillos; boil for 10 minutes.

2. Drain and take out stems; set aside until needed. Then heat a skillet over a medium flame and add oil.

3. Put in chicken and cook until browned.

4. Remove chicken from pan wand put on paper towels to remove excess oil. Put chicken back into pan and add onion, spices, carrots and spinach. Cook for 15 minutes till vegetables get a little soft.

5. Make sauce by blending serrano peppers and tomatillos along with garlic, onion and salt. Take seeds from poblano peppers and fill with beef mixture and drizzle sauce on top. Put leftover sauce into baking crock-pot and place peppers into pot.

6. Set pot on low and cook for 1 hour. Top with avocado and serve.

Nutritional Information (for chicken)

- Calories 352

- Fat 9.3 g

- Carbohydrates 17.5 g

- Protein 43.6 g

Peach Balsamic Rosemary Chicken

Serves: 6-8

Preparation Time: 3-4 hours

Ingredients

- Olive oil (2 tablespoons)

- Fresh rosemary (4 sprigs)

- Pepper (1/4 teaspoon)

- Honey (1/4 cup)

- Chicken thighs (10, skinless)

- Sweet Onion (1, sliced)

- Coarse salt (1 ½ teaspoons)

- Peaches (3, sliced and pitted

- Balsamic vinegar (3/4 cup)

Directions

1. Heat oil in pan and sauté rosemary, pepper, onion and salt together for 5 minutes.

2. Put in peaches and cook for 5 more minutes.

3. Add in vinegar and honey and boil until bubbly and sauce gets slightly thickened.

4. Put chicken into crock-pot and pour sauce on top of chicken. Put peaches evenly over chicken.

5. Set crockpot on high and cook for 3-4 hours.

6. Remove liquid from pot and put chicken aside till needed.

7. Pour into a saucepan. Cook sauce until it thickens then pour over chicken and serve.

Nutritional Information

- Calories 170

- Fat 3.8 g

- Saturated Fat 0.9 g

- Carbohydrates 22.7 g

- Protein 9.8 g

Crockpot Cauliflower Bolognese With Zucchini Noodle

Serves: 5-6

Preparation Time: 3 hours 40 minutes

Ingredients

- Cauliflower (1 head, chopped)

- Garlic (2 cloves, diced)

- Basil Flakes (1 teaspoon, dried)

- Vegetable broth (1/2 cup)

- Pepper

- Red onion (3/4 cup, chopped)

- Oregano (2 teaspoons, dried)

- Canned Tomatoes (3 ½ cups, diced)

- Red Pepper flakes (1/4 teaspoon)

Pasta:

- Zucchinis (5)

Directions

1. Put all the ingredients into Crockpot and set your pot on high.

2. Cook for 3 1/2hours.

3. Mash cooked cauliflower and stir together.

4. Serve with zucchini noodles.

Pasta:

- Use a slicer to strip zucchinis.

Nutritional Information

- Calories 210

- Fat 1.8 g

- Saturated Fat 0.5 g

- Carbohydrates 21.5 g

- Sugar 10.6 g

- Protein 3.8 g

Paleo Crockpot Cashew Chicken

Serves: 4-6

Preparation Time: 3-4 hours

Ingredients

- Arrowroot starch (1/4 cup)

- Chicken thighs (2 lbs, cut up)

- Coconut aminos (3 tablespoons)

- Tomato paste (2 tablespoons)

- Garlic (2 cloves, diced)

- Red Pepper flakes (1/2 teaspoon)

- Raw Cashews (1/2 cup)

- Black pepper (1/2 teaspoon)

- Coconut oil (1 tablespoon)

- Rice wine vinegar (2 tablespoons)

- Palm sugar (1 tablespoon)

- Fresh ginger (1/2 teaspoon, diced)

Directions

1. Put black pepper and arrowroot in a large plastic back. Put chicken in bag and shake until chicken is coated.

2. Heat coconut oil in a big skillet and cook chicken for 5 minutes until golden.

3. Put chicken into crock pot.

4. Combine vinegar, sugar, pepper flakes, aminos, tomato paste, garlic and ginger in a bowl and pour on top of chicken.

5. Set crock pot on low and cook for 3-4 hours.

6. Toss in cashews and combine then serve.

Nutritional Information

- Calories 260

- Fat 10.5 g

- Saturated Fat 1.5 g

- Carbohydrates 17.5 g

- Sugar 6.4 g

- Protein 18 g

Crockpot Chicken and Okra

Serves: 8

Preparation Time: 4 hours 45 minutes

Ingredients

- Chicken leg quarters (4)

- Black pepper (1/2 teaspoon)

- Garlic (4 cloves, diced)

- Italian seasoning (1 ½ teaspoon, dried)

- Canned Tomatoes (3 ½ cups, diced)

- Bell peppers (2, sliced and seeds removed)

- Flat leaf Parsley (1/2 cup, chopped)

- Salt (3/4 teaspoon)

- Canola (3 teaspoons)

- Onion (2, sliced)

- Red wine (1/2 cup, dry)

- Green olives (1/3 cup, chopped)

- Okra (3 cups, sliced)

Directions

1. Separate leg from thigh and remove the excess skin from bottom of the leg. Season with ¼ teaspoon pepper.

2. Heat 2 teaspoons of oil in a pot and cook chicken for 4 minutes on each side. Repeat until all the chicken is cooked.

3. Put browned chicken into crock pot.

4. Heat oil in skillet and sauté onion and garlic. Put in leftover pepper and Italian seasoning. Cook till veggies are browned and pour on top of chicken in crock pot.

5. Put tomato paste and wine into skillet and bring to a boil. Then pour on top of chicken and onions.

6. Put in peppers and set on high. Cook for 3 ½ hours, covered.

7. Remove cover and add in okra and cook for 30 additional minutes.

8. Put chicken into bowl and stir veggies together and spoon mixture into bowl. Garnish with parsley.

Nutritional Information

- Calories 252

- Fat 15.5 g

- Saturated Fat 4.5 g

- Carbohydrates 10 g

- Protein 1.6 g

Turkey Soup

Serves: 4-6

Preparation Time: 4 hours 30 minutes

Ingredients

- Olive oil (1 tablespoon)

- Cumin (2 tablepoons)

- Garlic powder (1/2 teaspoon)

- Turkey broth (5 cups)

- Canned tomatoes (3 ½ cups, diced)

- Cooked Turkey (2 cups, chopped)

- Onion (1/2, diced)

- Oregano (1/2 tablespoon)

- Parsley (1 tablespoon)

- Tomato paste (3/4 cup)

- Bell peppers (2, diced)

- Avocado

- Cilantro

Directions

1. Set Crockpot on low and put in all ingredients and stir.

2. Cook for 8 hours.

3. Serve topped with avocado and cilantro.

Nutritional Information

- Calories 122

- Fat 5 g

- Saturated Fat 0.5 g

- Carbohydrates 9.3 g

- Sugar 0.3 g

- Protein 4.6 g

Italian Meatballs

Serves: 4-6

Preparation Time: 4-6 hours

Ingredients

- Veggie mince (1 lb)

- Onion (1/2 cup, chopped)

- Italian seasoning (1 tablespoon)

- Garlic (1 tablespoon, diced)

- Tomatoes *3 ½ cups, crushed)

- Turkey sausage (1 lb)

- Almond flour (1/4 cup)

- Basil (1 tablespoon)

Directions

1. Combine all the ingredients in a big bowl excluding tomatoes.

2. Roll into balls and oil crock pot.

3. Put meatballs into crock pot and pour tomatoes along with more seasonings on top of meatballs.

4. Set on high and cook for 4 hours.

5. Serve with salad or other preferred side dish.

Nutritional Information

- Calories 141.7

- Fat 7.5 g

- Saturated Fat 2.4 g

- Carbohydrates 4.3 g

- Sugar 0.3 g

- Protein 8.6 g

Honey Mustard Chicken

Serves: 4-6

Preparation Time: 6hours

Ingredients

- Chicken breasts (6, whole)

- Honey (1/4 cup)

- Dijon mustard (1/2 cup)

- Chicken broth (1/2 cup)

- Dried herbs (1teaspoon)

Directions

1. Mix together mustard, honey and broth.

2. Put chicken into mixture and coat. Then put chicken into crock pot.

3. Pour leftover mix onto chicken and set pot on high.

4. Cook for 3 hours then set on low and cook for an additional 3 hours.

5. Sprinkle with dried herbs before serving.

Brazilian Curry Chicken

Serves: 4-6

Preparation Time: 4-5 hours

Ingredients

- Chicken breasts (1 1/2lbs)

- Chicken broth (3/4 cup)

- Garlic (2 cloves, diced)

- Curry powder (4 ½ tablespoons)

- Yellow Onion (3/4,sliced)

- Red pepper flakes

- Coconut milk (1 cup)

- Tomato paste (1 ½ tablespoons)

- Ground ginger (3/4 tablespoon)

- Bell peppers (1 ½)

- Black Pepper

Directions

1. Cut chicken into halves and put into crock pot.

2. Mix together tomato paste, curry powder, pepper, coconut milk, garlic, black pepper and ginger.

3. Pour mixture over chicken along with broth and bell peppers. Stir to combine.

4. Set pot to high and cook for 4-5 hours.

5. Serve with your desired side dish and enjoy.

Nutritional Information

- Calories 425.2

- Fat 20.3 g

- Saturated Fat 9.5 g

- Carbohydrates 37.4 g

- Sugar 23.4 g

- Protein 28.4 g

Chocolate Chicken Mole

Serves: 6

Preparation Time: 4-6 hours

Ingredients

- Chicken breasts (2lbs, skinned)

- Ghee (2 tablespoons)

- Garlic (4 cloves, crushed)

- Onion (1, chopped)

- Chipotles (5, chopped)

- Tomatoes (7, seeds removed and diced)

- Dark chocolate (2 ½ oz)

- Cumin (1 teaspoon)

- Chili powder- (1/2 teaspoon)

- Cinnamon (1/2 teaspoon)

- Jalapeno (chopped)

- Cilantro (chopped)

- Avocado (chopped)

Directions

1. Season chicken with pepper.

2. Heat a pan and add ghee. Put chicken into pan and brown all over.

3. Remove from pan and put into crock pot.

4. Return pan to flame and sauté onion and garlic. Add cooked onion and garlic to chicken in pot.

5. Add the rest of the ingredients to crock pot except cilantro, jalapeno and avocado.

6. Set pot to low and cook for 4-6 hours until chicken can be pulled apart.

7. Serve topped with jalapeno, cilantro and avocado.

Nutritional Information

- Calories 625.2

- Fat 42.3 g

- Saturated Fat 11.5 g

- Carbohydrates 27.4 g

- Sugar 13.4 g

- Protein 48.4 g

Crockpot BBQ Turkey Thighs

Serves: 2-4

Preparation Time: 6-8 hours

Ingredients

- Turkey thighs (2, large)

- Black pepper

- Dried herbs

- Paleo BBQ peach sauce

Paleo BBQ Peach Sauce

- Shallot (1/4 cup, chopped)

- Tomato paste (2 ¼ cups)

- Water (1/4 cup)

- Coconut aminos (2 teaspoons)

- Pepper (1/4 teaspoon)

- Peaches (1 cup, sliced)

- Apple cider vinegar (1/4 cup)

- Chipotle (1/4 teaspoon)

- Olive oil (1 teaspoon)

Directions

Making sauce:

1.   Cook shallots in oil for 5 minutes.

2.   Add in all other ingredients and cook for 5 additional minutes.

3.   Remove from pan and blend till mixture is smooth.

Turkey

1.   Season turkey with herbs and pepper and put into crockpot.

2.   Put in bbq sauce and set pot on low.

3.   Cook for 6-8 hours.

Nutritional Information

- Calories 610.2

- Fat 40.3 g

- Saturated Fat 12.5 g

- Carbohydrates 13.4 g

- Sugar 6.4 g

- Protein 68.4 g

Tomato, Basil and Tofu Soup

Serves: 4

Preparation Time: 3-4hours

Ingredients

- Coconut milk (1 cup)

- Canned tomatoes (2 ¾ cups, diced)

- Coconut oil (1 tablespoon)

- Tofu (1 lb, cubed)

- Chicken broth (1 cup)

- Onion (1 cup, chopped)

- Garlic (3 cloves, diced)

- Basil (1/4 cup, chopped)

Directions

1. Blend together coconut milk and tomatoes and pour into crockpot.

2. Put in remaining ingredients and stir to combine.

3. Set pot on low and cook for 3-4 hours.

4. Add basil right before serving.

Paleo Stuffed Peppers

Serves: 2-4

Preparation Time: 6 hours

Ingredients

- Chicken (1lb, shredded)

- Cauliflower (1/2, chopped)

- Onion (1, diced)

- Basil (2 teaspoons)

- Thyme (2 teaspoons, dried)

- Bell peppers (6)

- Tomato paste (1 cup)

- Garlic (3 cloves, diced)

- Oregano (2 teaspoons)

Directions

1. Cut the top of the peppers off and remove the seeds.

2. Use a processor to chop cauliflower until it has a rice like texture.

3. Put into a bowl along with chicken, onion, tomato paste garlic, herbs and basil and mix together with hands.

4. Use a spoon to fill peppers and place them into crock pot. You may put any left over mixture into crock pot between peppers.

5. Set pot to low and cook for 6 hours.

Nutritional Information

- Calories 152.2

- Fat 8.6 g

- Saturated Fat 0.5 g

- Carbohydrates 14.3 g

- Sugar 4.7 g

- Protein 16.4 g

Roasted Asparagus Avocado Soup

Serves: 2-4

Preparation Time: 2-3 hours

Ingredients

- Asparagus (1/2 cups)

- Vegetable broth (2 cups)

- Lemon juice

- Ghee (1 tablespoon)

- Olive oil

- Garlic

- Avocado (1, cubed)

- Pepper

Directions

1. Heat oil in pan and sauté until garlic is fragrant.

2. Put half of asparagus into blender with all leftover ingredients.

3. Put mixture into crock pot along with garlic and remaining asparagus, set on low and cook for 2-3 hours.

4. Add water if necessary and heat thoroughly.

Nutritional Information

- Calories 252.2

- Fat 23.6 g

- Saturated Fat 12.6 g

- Carbohydrates 11.4 g

- Sugar 6.7 g

- Protein 3.4 g

Crockpot Squash Chili

Serves: 6

Preparation Time: 8- 10 hours

Ingredients

- Ground turkey (1 lb)

- Garlic (3 cloves, diced)

- Ground cumin (1 teaspoon)

- Squash (2 ½ lbs)

- Tomato paste (3/4 cup)

- Onion (1 cup, minced)

- Chili powder (2 tablespoons)

- Oregano (1/2 teaspoon)

- Whole tomatoes (2 cups)

Directions

1. Put turkey, garlic, spices and onions into crock pot. Stir mixture together and break turkey into smaller pieces.

2. Peel and cut squash into quarters then slice into chunks. Place on top of turkey.

3. Pulse tomato paste and tomatoes in a blender and pour onto squash.

4. Set Crockpot on low and cook for 8 to 10 hours.

5. Serve with desired toppings.

Nutritional Information

- Calories 352.2

- Fat 9.6 g

- Saturated Fat 2.6 g

- Carbohydrates 51.4 g

- Sugars 9.7 g

- Protein 1 .4 g

Slow Cooker Orange Chicken

Serves: 4-6

Preparation Time: 4-6 hours

Ingredients

- Chicken breasts (2 lbs, cubed)

- Ginger (1 tablespoon, grated)

- Garlic)3 cloves, crushed)

- Chili flakes (1 teaspoon)

- Honey (3 tablespoons)

- Sesame oil (2 teaspoons)

- Onion (1, diced)

- Orange juice (from 1 freshly squeezed orange)

- Orange rind

- Chicken broth (1/4 cup)

- Apple cider vinegar (1 ½ tablespoons)

- Paprika (1/2 teaspoon)

- Sesame seeds (1 tablespoon)

Directions

1. Put chicken into crock pot.

2. Mix all ingredients together except sesame seeds and oil.

3. Pour on top of chicken and set crock pot on low.

4. Cook for 4-6 hours and stir in sesame seeds.

5. Serve with desired side dish.

Nutritional Information

- Calories 288

- Fat 5.2 g

- Saturated Fat 1.6 g

- Carbohydrates 30.4 g

- Sugars 19.7 g

- Protein 24 g

Crockpot Honey Garlic Wings

Serves: 4-6

Preparation Time: 5-6 hours

Ingredients

- Chicken wings (2 lbs)

- Garlic (1 ½ tablespoons)

- Black Pepper (1/2 teaspoon)

- Honey (3/4 cup)

- Olive oil (2 tablespoons)

- Cayenne Pepper (2 tablespoons)

Directions

1. Put wings into crock pot.

2. Mix remaining ingredients in a bowl and pour on top wings. Mix wings and honey blend together.

3. Set crock pot on low and cook for 4-6 hours.

Nutritional Information

- Calories 312.2

- Fat 8.6 g

- Carbohydrates 50.3 g

Crock Pot Moroccan Chicken

Serves: 6-8

Preparation Time: 6-8 hours

Ingredients

- Canned Tomato Sauce (1 ¾ cups)

- Lemon juice

- Ground Ginger (1 teaspoon)

- Sweet Paprika (1/2 teaspoon)

- Onions (2, sliced)

- Ginger (1 tablespoon, grated)

- Almond butter (1/3 cup)

- Coconut oil (3 tablespoons)

- Apricot puree (1/3 cup)

- Cumin (1 teaspoon)

- Chicken thighs (4 lbs)

- Garlic (3 cloves, diced)

- Cinnamon sticks (3)

- Water (2 cups)

Directions

1. Mix together apricot puree, cumin, paprika, tomato sauce, lemon juice and ground ginger in a bowl.

2. Heat oil in a large frying pan and cook chicken for 4 minutes on each side.

3. Take chicken from pan and put into crock pot.

4. Sauté ginger, onion and garlic and add to crock pot.

5. Put tomato sauce into pan along with water and butter. Stir and pour onto chicken in crock pot.

6. Set crock pot on low and add cinnamon.

7. Cook for 6-8 hours.

Nutritional Information

- Calories 340.8

- Fat 10.5 g

- Saturated Fat 1.5 g

- Carbohydrates 60.3 g

- Sugars 26.7 g

- Protein 24 g

Crockpot Italian Tofu Stew

Serves: 8

Preparation Time: 8-10 hours

Ingredients

- Olive oil (4 tablespoons)

- Tofu (1 lb)

- Carrots (2 cups, chopped)

- Onions (2, diced)

- Italian red wine (2 cups)

- Tomatoes (1 ¾ cups)

- Almond flour (1/3 cup)

- Mushrooms (1 lb)

- Oregano (1/2 teaspoon)

- Marjoram (1/2 teaspoon, dried)

- Black pepper

- Bay leaf (1)

- Celery (1 ½ cups, chopped)

- Garlic (3 cloves, diced)

- Beef broth (2 cups)

- Rosemary (3/4 teaspoon, dried)

Directions

1. Put oil into a pan and cook tofu for 10 minutes.

2. Add remaining oil and put in garlic, celery, carrots and onion. Cook for 15 minutes, stirring to avoid burning.

3. Pour in wine and mix to combine.

4. Pour into crock pot and put in remaining ingredients.

5. Set crock pot on low and cook for 8-10 hours.

Nutritional Information

- Calories 356

- Fat 14.6 g

- Saturated Fat 3.5 g

- Carbohydrates 33.3 g

- Sugars 16.7 g

- Protein 28 g

Slow Cooker Maple Glazed Pecans

Serves: 4-6

Preparation Time: 2 hours 10minutes

Ingredients

- Pecans (3 cups, raw)

- Vanilla extracts (2 teaspoons)

- Coconut oil (1 tablespoon)

- Maple syrup (1/4 cup)

Directions

1. Put all ingredients into crock pot.

2. Set to low and cook for 1-3 hours. Stir frequently to avoid burning.

3. Cool and store in a clean container, preferably made of glass.

Nutritional Information

- Calories 280

- Fat 11.6 g

- Saturated Fat 2.8 g

- Carbohydrates 45.3 g

- Sugars 21.7 g

- Protein 12.3 g

Creamy Pumpkin Soup

Serves: 4-6

Preparation Time: 5-6 hours

Ingredients

- Pumpkin (3 cups)

- Vegetable broth (4 cups)

- Coconut milk (2cups)

- Onion (1/2, chopped)

- Basil (1 tablespoon, dried)

- Garlic (1 clove, crushed)

- Carrots (1 cup, chopped)

- Black pepper

- Dried herbs (1-2 teaspoons)

Directions

1. Cut pumpkin into cubes and put into crock pot with broth.

2. Put in all other ingredients except coconut milk.

3. Set on low and cook for 5 hours.

4. Add milk and cook for another 30 minutes.

Crockpot Roasted Chicken with Lemon Parsley Butter

Serves: 6-8

Preparation Time: 3-4 hours

Ingredients

- Whole chicken (5 lbs)

- Dried herbs (1 teaspoon)

- Water (1 cup)

- Whole Lemon (thinly sliced)

- Parsley (2 tablespoons, chopped)

- Ghee (4 tablespoons)

Directions

1. Wash chicken and remove insides. Use hand towels to pat till dry.

2. Rub herbs and pepper onto chicken and put into crock pot.

3. Add water to pot and set on high.

4. Cook for 3 hours and test meat if it is cooked thoroughly. (be sure to add more water if necessary)

5. Top with lemon, butter and parsley and cover pot. Cook for an additional 30minutes.

Cream of Broccoli Soup

Serves: 4-6

Preparation Time: 3 hours

Ingredients

- Chicken broth (3 cups)

- Broccoli (3 cups, chopped)

- Coconut milk (2 cups)

- Onion (1, chopped)

- Black pepper (1/2 teaspoon)

- Dried herbs (1/2 teaspoon)

- Vegan plain cheese (1 cup, shredded)

- Scallions (chopped)

- Thyme (1/4 teaspoon)

Directions

1. Put all ingredients into pot except milk and cheese.

2. Set on high and cook for 2 hours, then add in milk.

3. Cook for an additional hour and top with cheese.

4. Serve and enjoy.

Greek Stuffed Chicken Breasts

Serves: 4-6

Preparation Time: 6-8 hours

Ingredients

- Chicken breasts (6, boneless)

- Onion (1, diced)

- Olive oil (1 tablespoon)

- Red Pepper (1/2 sliced)

- Spinach (3/4 cup)

- Oregano (1/2, dried)

- Black pepper

- Chicken broth (1 cup)

- White wine (1/2 cup)

- Vegan cheddar Cheese (1/3 cup)

- Lenon

- Garlic (2 teaspoons)

- Pepperoncini peppers (2, sliced)

Directions

1. Slit chicken breast and season with black pepper.

2. Cook onions and peppers for 2 minutes and then put in spinach and garlic. Cook till wilted then put in oregano.

3. Take pot from flame and stir in cheese.

4. Spoon mixture into chicken breasts and place them into a crock pot.

5. Squeeze lemon over chicken and add broth and wine.

6. Set crock pot on low and cook for 6-8 hours.

Nutritional Information

- Calories 670.5

- Fat 48.6 g

- Saturated Fat 12.5 g

- Carbohydrates 35.3 g

- Sugars 4.7 g

- Protein 44 g

Paleo Crockpot Jambalaya Soup

Serves: 4-6

Preparation Time: 5-6 hours

Ingredients

- Chicken broth (5 cups)

- Bell peppers (4, chopped

- Canned Tomatoes (2 cups, diced)

- Onion (1, chopped)

- Garlic (2 cloves, minced)

- Shrimp (1 lb, raw)

- Chicken (4 oz, diced)

- Bay leaves (2)

- Cauliflower (1 head)

- Okra (2 cups)

- Hot sauce (1/4 cup)

- Cajun Seasoning (3 tablespoons)

Directions

1. Put chicken broth along with hot sauce, bay leaves, chopped peppers, garlic, onion and chicken.

2. Set crock pot on low and cook for 5 hours.

3. Put cauliflower into food processor and blend until it resembles rice.

4. Put in shrimp and cauliflower and stir. Cook for 20 minutes and serve.

Nutritional Information

- Calories 270.5

- Fat 4.6 g

- Saturated Fat 0.7 g

- Carbohydrates 35.4 g

- Sugars 5.1 g

- Protein 24 g

Crockpot Spaghetti and Meat Balls

Serves: 2-4

Preparation Time: 3-4 hours

Ingredients

- Spaghetti squash (1)

- Ground turkey (1 lb)

- Garlic (4 cloves)

- Tomato sauce (1 ¾ cups)

- Italian seasoning (2 teaspoons)

- Hot pepper relish (2 tablespoons)

Directions

1. Put tomato sauce along with Italian seasoning, olive oil, relish and garlic into crockpot.

2. Cut squash in two and place opened sides down.

3. Roll your turkey into meat balls and put them into pot, around squash.

4. Set crock pot on high for 3 hours.

5. Remove squash and use a fork to pull insides out (spaghetti) and top with meatballs. You may add other toppings if you like.

Crockpot Barley Risotto

Serves: 4-6

Preparation Time: 6-8 hours

Ingredients

- Olive oil (1/2 tablespoon)

- Garlic (1 teaspoon, diced)

- Pearl barley (1 ½ cups)

- Pumpkin (2 cups)

- Onions (2 ½ onions)

- Rosemary (1/2 teaspoon, dried)

- Vegetable broth (3 cups)

Directions

1. Chop onions and pumpkin.

2. Heat oil in a skillet and cook onions for 2 minutes then add in rosemary and garlic and cook for 1 minute.

3. Put in barley and stir to combine.

4. Put mixture into crock pot and add broth.

5. Set crock-pot on low and cook for 6-8 hours.

6. Add pumpkin in the last 30 minutes of cooking.

Nutritional Information

- Calories 359.4

- Fat 2.6 g

- Saturated Fat 0.4 g

- Carbohydrates 77.2 g

- Sugars 5.6 g

- Protein 9 g

Crockpot Sweet and Sour Tofu

Serves: 6

Preparation Time: 3-4 hours

Ingredients

- Tofu (1 lb, extra firm)

- Olive oil (2 tablespoons)

- Bell pepper (1)

- Carrot (1 cup, sliced)

- Water chestnuts (1 cup, sliced)

- Water (1 tablespoon)

- Cornstarch (1 tablespoon)

- Onion (1/2, chopped)

- Broccoli (1 cup, florets)

- La Choy Sweet and sour sauce (1 ¼ cups)

Directions

1. Squeeze excess moisture from tofu and cube.

2. Put tofu along with cornstarch in a plastic bag and shake.

3. Heat oil in a skillet and take tofu from bad and place into oil. Cook for 15 minutes on all sides till a crust is formed.

4. Put vegetables and tofu into crock pot and add sweet and sour sauce. Use water to shake rest of sauce from jar.

5. Set crock pot on low and cook for 3 hours.

Nutritional Information

- Calories 197.7

- Fat 8.9 g

- Saturated Fat 1.4 g

- Carbohydrates 24.1 g

- Sugars 12.4 g

- Protein 7.6 g

Indian Style Curry Soup

Serves: 6-8

Preparation Time: 8-10 hours

Ingredients

- Eggplants (6 cup, cubed)

- Tomatoes (2 cups, chopped)

- Fresh ginger (1 tablespoon, grated)

- Ground coriander (1 ½ teaspoons)

- Black pepper (1/4 teaspoon)

- Cilantro (2 tablespoons, chopped)

- Garbanzo beans (2 cups)

- Mustard seeds (1 ½ teaspoons)

- Curry (1 teaspoon)

- Vegetable broth (4 cups)

Directions

1. Combine tomatoes, garbanzo beans and eggplant in a crock pot.

2. Sprinkle mustard seeds, curry, ginger, pepper and coriander on top of vegetables.

3. Add broth and set crock pot on low.

4. Cook for 8-10 hours.

5. Serve topped with cilantro.

Nutritional Information

- Calories 172.9

- Fat 1.5 g

- Saturated Fat 0.1 g

- Carbohydrates 35.1 g

- Sugars 4 g

- Protein 6.4 g

Crockpot Roasted Beets

Serves: 6

Preparation Time: 5 hours

Ingredients

- Beets (6)

- Soy margarine (1 teaspoon)

- Dried herbs

Directions

1. Scrub beets then get a piece of foil large enough for beet and add a little margarine then put in beet and wrap.

2. Put beets into crock pot.

3. Set on high and cook for 3-5 hours.

4. Pierce to check if done and slice.

Nutritional Information

- Calories 30

- Fat 0.6 g

- Carbohydrates 5.3 g

- Sugars 3.9 g

- Protein 0.8 g

Crockpot Red Beans and Rice

Serves: 2-4

Preparation Time: 2-3 hours

Ingredients

- Red beans (1 cup, dried)

- Bay leaves (4)

- Celery (3 stalks, chopped)

- Red Bell Pepper (1, seeds removed and chopped)

- Black Pepper

- Water (5 cups)

- Thyme (1 tablespoon)

- Onion (1, chopped)

- Red Pepper flakes (1 tablespoon)

Directions

1. Soak beans overnight.

2. Put soaked beans into a pot adding more water to make 5 cups.

3. Put in bay leaves and cook for 45 minutes till beans are soft.

4. Put chopped veggies into crock pot along with pepper flakes, thyme and black pepper.

5. Remove 2 cups of water from beans and put aside till needed.

6. Pour the rest of the beans and water into crock pot and add extra water to cover beans.

7. Set on high and cook for 2 hours. When veggies have gotten soft use spoon to mash mixture.

8. Simmer and serve with rice.

Nutritional Information

- Calories 470.5

- Fat 1.6 g

- Saturated Fat 0.2 g

- Carbohydrates 96.3 g

- Sugars 5.6 g

- Protein 15.6 g

Crockpot Bok Choy

Serves: 4-6 hours

Preparation Time: 4 hours

Ingredients

- Soy sauce (2 tablespoons)

- Mirin (1 tablespoon)

- Peanut oil (1 tablespoon)

- Ginger (1 teaspoon, diced)

- Scallions (3, sliced)

- Hoisin sauce (1 tablespoon)

- Water (1 tablespoon)

- Garlic (1, diced)

- Baby Bok Choy (3 heads, cut into halves)

Directions

1. Combine hoisin sauce, water, tamari and mirin and put aside.

2. Put oil in crock pot and add ginger and garlic.

3. Put in bok choy and top with scallions and pour liquid on top.

4. Set pot on low and cook for 4 hours.

Crockpot Artichokes

Serves: 4

Preparation Time: 4 hours

Ingredients

- Artichokes (4)

- Lemon juice (1 tablespoon)

- Butter (melted)

- Water

Directions

1. Remove bottom stem off of artichokes and cut an inch from top.

2. Wash and place them into crock-pot standing up.

3. Fill water, half way covering artichokes and add in lemon juice.

4. Spoon some water from pan into top of artichokes.

5. Set pot on high and cook for 4 hours.

Nutritional Information

- Calories 61

- Fat 0.1 g

- Carbohydrates 13.7 g

- Protein 4.2 g

Crockpot Ratatouille with Chickpeas

Serves: 6

Preparation Time: 4-5 hours

Ingredients

- Vegetable oil (1 tablespoon)

- Garlic (4 cloves, diced)

- Bail (2 teaspoons, dried)

- Pepper (1/2 teaspoon)

- Bell Pepper (2)

- Tomato paste (1/3 cup)

- Canned Tomatoes (3 1/2 cups)

- Onion (1, chopped)

- Eggplants (6 cups, cubed)

- Oregano (1 teaspoon, dried)

- Black pepper (1/2 teaspoon)

- Zucchini (2)

- Chickpeas (2 ¼ cups, drained and washed)

- Parsley (1/4 cup, chopped)

Directions

1. Heat oil in a large skillet and sauté garlic, oregano, onion, eggplant and black pepper together. Cook for 10 minutes.

2. Put mixture into crock pot. Cut peppers into halves and remove seeds. Slice zucchini in half then cut across and put into pot.

3. Add chickpeas, tomatoes and tomato paste into pot. Crush tomatoes and set pot on low.

4. Cook for 4 hours then add parsley.

Nutritional Information

- Calories 219.5

- Fat 4.1 g

- Saturated Fat 0.5 g

- Carbohydrates 40.6 g

- Sugars 10.4 g

- Protein 8.7 g

Mediterranean Style Means and Vegetables

Serves: 6

Preparation Time: 8 hours 15 minutes

Ingredients

- Canned great northern beans (2 cups)

- Garlic (5 teaspoons, minced)

- Carrot (1 cup, sliced)

- Green beans (2 cups, cut)

- Bay leaves (2)

- Pepper

- Canned Red beans (2 cups)

- Onion (1, chopped)

- Celery (1/2 cup, sliced)

- Red chili peppers (2, seeds removed)

Directions

1. Put all ingredients into a crockpot.

2. Set crock pot on low and cook for 8 hours

3. Take bay leaves out of pot and serve.

Sweet and Sour Cabbage

Serves: 6

Preparation: 8 hours

Ingredients

- Red Cabbage (1 head, shredded)

- Balsamic vinegar (3 tablespoons)

- Molasses (1 tablespoon)

- Apples (3, chopped)

- Water (3 tablespoons)

- Honey (1/2 cup)

Directions

1. Put apples and cabbage into crock pot.

2. Mix remaining ingredients together and pour on top cabbage.

3. Set crock pot on low and cook for 8 hours.

Nutritional Information

- Calories 171.8

- Fat 3 g

- Carbohydrates 43.3 g

- Protein 2.2 g

Sweet Acorn Squash with Apples

Serves: 4

Preparation Time: 4 hours 15 minutes

Ingredients

- Apple cider vinegar (1/2 cup)

- Vegan margarine (2 tablespoons)

- Cranberries (1/4 cup, dried)

- Lemon juice

- Maple syrup (2 tablespoons)

- Acorn squash (1, cut into quarters)

- Honey (2 tablespoons)

- Apples (1 ½ cup, chopped)

- Cinnamon (1 teaspoon)

- Walnuts (3 tablespoons)

Directions

1. Set crock pot on high and pour in vinegar.

2. Put in squash with cut side facing up.

3. Top with ½ tablespoon honey, ½ tablespoon butter and 1 teaspoon cranberries.

4. Drop in apples all over squash.

5. Put in lemon juice, maple syrup and cinnamon.

6. Set on low and cook for 4-6hours.

7. Serve with nuts.

Nutritional Information

- Calories 225.7

- Fat 9.5 g

- Saturated Fat 4 g

- Carbohydrates 37 g

- Sugars 21 g

- Protein 2 g

Crockpot Winter Vegetable Casserole

Serves: 4

Preparation Time: 4 hours 15 minutes

Ingredients

- Dry cider (400 ml)

- Leeks (3, sliced)

- Parsnips (3, cut up)

- Swede (1, cut up)

- Bay leaves (3)

- Vegetable broth (250 ml)

- Carrots (3, chopped)

- Turnip (1, chopped)

- Cauliflower (1 head, chopped)

Directions

1. Put vinegar into crock pot and cover.

2. Set pot to high and add in bay leaves and vegetables.

3. Cook for 4 hours.

Crockpot Red Lentil Dahl

Serves: 4-6

Preparation Time: 8 hours

Ingredients

- Red Lentils (2 cups, dried)

- Ginger (2 tablespoons, diced)

- Curry powder (1 tablespoon)

- Ground Coriander (1 teaspoon)

- Red pepper flakes

- Vegetable broth (4 cups)

- Garlic (4 cloves, diced)

- Spinach (1 ¼ cups)

- Ground cumin (1 teaspoon)

- Yellow mustard seeds (1 teaspoon)

- Ground cinnamon

- Water

Directions

1. Put all ingredients into pot and set on low.

2. Cook for 6-8 hours. Check on water to make sure it does not burn.

Nutritional Information

- Calories 377

- Fat 2.0 g

- Saturated Fat 0.2 g

- Carbohydrates 63.5 g

- Sugars 2.5 g

- Protein 28.2 g

Rice and Raisin-Stuffed Cabbage Rolls

Serves: 6

Preparation Time: 6 hours 30 minutes

Ingredients

- Green cabbage (1 head, cored)

- Onion (1, chopped)

- Fresh Parsley leaves (2 tablespoons, chopped)

- Ground allspice (1/4 teaspoon)

- Cayenne pepper (1/8 teaspoon)

- Brown rice (3 cups, cooked)

- Water (3/4 cup)

- Olive oil (2 tablespoons)

- Raisins (1/2 cup, soaked for 10 minutes in warm water)

- Honey (1 teaspoon)

- Ground Cinnamon (1/8 teaspoon)

- Black Pepper

- Lemon juice (1 tablespoon, fresh)

- Apple juice (3/4 cup)

Directions

1. Put cabbage in a large pot and steam for 10 minutes.

2. Heat half of oil in a skillet and cook onion for 5 minutes. Put in parsley, allspice, raisins, cinnamon and honey.

3. Stir mixture and put in black pepper and cayenne pepper. Put rice into mixture along with lemon juice.

4. Remove soft leaves from cabbage and lay them flat.

5. Stuff each leaf with rice stuffing and roll leaves. Steam more leaves if necessary.

6. Put stuffed cabbages into crock pot and pour remaining oil, apple juice and water over them.

7. Set crock pot on low and cook for 6-8 hours.

Nutritional Information

- Calories 261.5

- Fat 5.6 g

- Saturated Fat 0.8 g

- Carbohydrates 50.6 g

- Sugars 19.5 g

- Protein 5.8 g

Mexicali Rice

Serves: 4

Preparation Time: 3 hours

Ingredients

- Canned Whole kernel corn (2 cups)

- Canned green chilies (1/2 cup)

- Bell pepper- red (1, chopped)

- Boiling water (3 ½ cups)

- Lime juice (6 tablespoons, fresh)

- Chili powder (1 tablespoon)

- Canned black beans (2 cups)

- Onion (1, chopped)

- Brown rice (2 cups)

- Orange juice concentrate (1/2 cup)

- Ground cumin (1 ½ tablespoons)

- Cilantro (1/3 cup, chopped)

Directions

1. Put all ingredients into crock pot except cilantro and lime juice.

2. Set on low and cook for 3 hours.

3. Put in cilantro and lime juice. Mix to combine.

4. Serve immediately.

Nutritional Information

- Calories 636.6

- Fat 5.2 g

- Saturated Fat 0.9 g

- Carbohydrates 134 g

- Sugars 20.6 g

- Protein 19.5 g

Corn Chowder

Serves: 4-6

Preparation Time: 6-7 hours

Ingredients

- Olive oil (tablespoon)

- Celery (1 rib, diced)

- Corn (3 cups)

- Vegetable broth (4 cups)

- Tomato (1, seeds removed and chopped)

- Onion (1, chopped)

- Coconut cream (1 cup)

- Bell Pepper- yellow (1/2, seeds removed, chopped)

- Pepper

- Chives (1 tablespoon)

Directions

1. Heat oil in pan and cook celery and onion for 5 minutes till they are soft.

2. Put celery and onion along with remaining ingredients except coconut cream into crock pot.

3. Set on low and cook for 6 hours.

4. Puree soup and return to crock pot. Add in coconut cream and heat for 30 minutes.

5. Serve topped with chives and tomatoes.

Nutritional Information

- Calories 217.4

- Fat 5.1 g

- Saturated Fat 0.7 g

- Carbohydrates 43.4 g

- Sugars 6.3 g

- Protein 5.6 g

Spiced Curried Lentil Stew with Cashew Nuts

Serves: 4-6

Preparation Time: 2 hours 20 minutes

Ingredients

- Olive oil (1/4 cup)

- Garlic (3 gloves, diced)

- Curry powder (1 tablespoon)

- Ground coriander (1 teaspoon)

- Tomatoes (2, seeds removed, chopped)

- Vegetable broth (4 cups)

- Cardamom pods (2)

- Zucchini (3, diced)

- Black Pepper

- Onions (2, chopped)

- Jalapeno (1, seeded removed and minced)

- Ground cumin (1 teaspoon)

- Turmeric (1/2 teaspoon)

- Brown Lentils (1 ½ cups)

- Cinnamon sticks (2)

- Cashew nuts (1 cup)

- Fresh cilantro (1/4cup, chopped)

Directions

1. Heat oil in a skillet and cook jalapeno, onions and garlic for 3 minutes. Put in cumin, turmeric, curry and coriander.

2. Put mixture into crock pot. Add lentils, cinnamon sticks, tomatoes and broth.

3. Set pot on low and cook for 3-5 hours.

4. Put cashews into oven on a lined baking sheet, for 7minutes.

5. Take cardamom and cinnamon from pot and put in cilantro and zucchini.

6. Cook for an additional 30 minutes and serve hot with desired side dish.

Nutritional Information

- Calories 642.1

- Fat 31.2 g

- Saturated Fat 5.3 g

- Carbohydrates 69.1 g

- Protein 27.3 g

Crockpot Vegan Tangine

Serves: 6

Preparation Time: 6 hours 45 minutes

Ingredients

- Parsnip (1/2 lb,chopped)

- Onions (2, diced)

- Apricots-dried (12, chopped)

- Ground turmeric (1 teaspoon)

- Ground ginger (1/2 teaspoon)

- Cayenne pepper (1/4 teaspoon)

- Cilantro-dried (1 tablespoon)

- Turnip (1/2 lb, chopped)

- Carrot (1/2 lb, diced)

- Prunes (12, pits removed and chopped)

- Ground cumin (2 teaspoons)

- Ground cinnamon (1 teaspoon)

- Parsley-dried (1 tablespoon)

- Vegetable broth (4 cups)

Directions

1. Put turnips, carrots, prunes, parsnips, onions and apricots in crock pot.

2. Add cumin, cinnamon, parsley. Cilantro, turmeric, ginger and cayenne. Toss and add broth.

3. Set on low and cook for 6 hours.

Nutritional Information

- Calories 155.9

- Fat 0.6 g

- Saturated Fat 0.1 g

- Carbohydrates 38.5 g

- Sugars 21.4 g

- Protein 2.7 g

Spicy Chicken Drumsticks

Ingredients

- **Nonstick Spray for Cooking**
- **1 Pound of Chicken Drumsticks (Approximately: 4 Drumsticks)**
- **½ cup Bottled Picante Sauce**
- **2 tsp. of Bottled Cayenne Pepper Sauce (For example: Franks Red Hot or 1/8 tsp. of Cayenne Pepper)**
- **½ tsp. Smoked Paprika**
- **¼ tsp. Dried and Crushed Thyme**
- **1 Bay Leaf**
- **2 tsp. of Olive Oil**

Directions

1. Coat a cool, unheated 3-quart or 3 ½ quart slow cooker with the spray.
2. In a small mixing bowl, add the pepper sauce, paprika, picante sauce, thyme, and the bay leaf.
3. Place the drumsticks into the slow cooker.
4. Spoon the pepper mix over the chicken drumsticks.
5. Cover the chicken and cook it on low heat for six hours. (Or on high heat for three hours.)
6. After cooking time, transfer the drumsticks to a serving dish.
7. Remove the bay leaf for the sauce that was left in the slow cooker and stir in the oil.
8. Spoon the sauce over the chicken evenly.

9. Allow it to stand for 10 minutes. This will allow the flavors to absorb into the chicken better.

10. Place a serving on a plate and spoon over 1 tsp. onto the drumstick. Get rid of any sauce that is left over.

Nutritional Information per serving

- Calories: 209
- Total Fat: 2g
- Saturated Fat: 2g
- Carbohydrates: 3g
- Protein: 27g

Ingredients

- **6 Cups Peeled and Cut (3/4 inch cubes) of Potatoes**
- **1 Cup Water**
- **2/3 Cup of Cider Vinegar**
- **¼ Cup of Sweetener**
- **1 Cup of Onion - Chopped**
- **2 Tbsp. of Quick Cooking Tapioca**
- **Dash of Salt**
- **¼ tsp. of Celery Seeds**
- **¼ tsp. of Ground Black Pepper**
- **4 Slices of Turkey Bacon (Cook the turkey bacon according to the package, and chop.)**

Directions

1. In a 3-½ quart or 4-quart slow cooker, combine the onion and potatoes.
2. In a medium-mixing bowl, add the cider vinegar, water, tapioca, sweetener, celery seeds, salt, and pepper; mix thoroughly.
3. Pour the potatoes into the slow cooker.
4. Cover the potatoes and cook them on low heat for 8-9 hours or on high heat for 4 to 4 ½ hours.
5. Stir in the bacon and serve.

Nutritional Information per serving

- Calories: 148
- Total Fat: 1g
- Saturated Fat: 0g
- Carbohydrates: 31g
- Protein: 3g

Vegetable Stew and Curried Chicken

Ingredients
- 1 – 16 Ounce Package of Frozen Stew Vegetables
- 4 Chicken Thighs – Large (Skinned)
- ¼ tsp. of Black Pepper
- 1 – 10 ¾ Ounce Can of Reduced Fat and Reduced Sodium Condensed Cream of Chicken Soup
- 2 tsp. of Curry Powder
- 1 Tbsp. of Fresh Cilantro – Snipped

Directions
1. Put the stew vegetables in a 4-quart slow cooker.
2. Top it with the chicken.
3. Sprinkle the pepper onto the chicken.
4. In a small mixing bowl, add the soup and the curry powder.
5. Pour the soup mixtures onto the chicken.
6. Cover the chicken and allow it to cook on low heat for 6-7 hours or on high heat for 3 – 3 ½ hours.
7. Remove the chicken bones.
8. Break the large chicken pieces into smaller ones.
9. Add a dash of fresh cilantro to the top of each serving.

Nutritional Information
- Calories: 299
- Total Fat: 2g
- Saturated Fat: 2g
- Carbohydrates: 19g
- Protein: 35g

Slow Roasted Savory Tomatoes

Ingredients

- **Cooking Spray**
- **2 Large Ripe Tomatoes (Cut in half crosswise)**
- **1 Tbsp. of Balsamic Vinegar**
- **2 tsp. of Olive Oil**
- **2 Minced Cloves of Garlic**
- **1 tsp. of Dried Basil (Crushed)**
- **¼ tsp. of Dried Rosemary (Crushed)**
- **½ tsp. of Dried Rosemary (Crushed)**
- **Dash of Salt**
- **¾ Cup of Course Whole Wheat Bread Crumbs (1 – slice)**
- **2 Tbsp. of Parmesan Cheese (Grated)**
- **Fresh Basil – Snipped**

Directions

1. Coat an unheated 3-½ quart slow cooker with the cooking spray.
2. Put the cut up tomatoes in the cooker. (Cut sides up.)
3. In a small mixing bowl, mix in the oil, garlic, vinegar, basil, oregano, salt, and rosemary.
4. Spoon the mixture over the tomatoes.
5. Cover the tomatoes and allow it to cook on low heat for 2 hours or on high heat for 1 hour.
6. Preheat a nonstick pan over medium heat.
7. Add the breadcrumbs and allow them to cook for 2-3 minutes. (Stir consistently.)
8. Remove the breadcrumbs from the heat and stir in the Parmesan.
9. To serve the tomatoes, remove them from the cooker and place them in a serving dish.

10. Drizzle the liquid over the tomatoes and sprinkle them with the Parmesan Cheese mixture. Garnish with the fresh basil.

Nutritional Information

- Calories: 96
- Total Fat: 1g
- Saturated Fat: 1g
- Carbohydrates: 13g
- Protein: 3g

Delicious Spicy Tomato Dip

Ingredients

- 1 – 15 Ounce Can of No Salt Added Tomato Sauce
- 1 – 14 ½ Ounce Can of No Salt Added Tomatoes (Diced)
- 1 Medium Finely Chopped Onion
- 3 Ounces of No Salt Added Tomato Paste
- 1 ½ tsp. of Crushed Dried Oregano
- 1 ½ tsp. of Dried Crushed Basil
- 2 Cloves of Minced Garlic
- 1 tsp. of Sugar
- 1/8 tsp. of Cayenne Pepper
- 3 Tbsp. of Chopped and Pitted Olives

Directions

1. In a 2-quart slow cooker, add tomatoes, tomato sauce, tomato paste, onion, basil, oregano, sugar, garlic, and cayenne pepper.
2. Cover the mixture and cook it on low heat for 5-6 hours.
3. Stir in the olives.
4. Serve is warm with vegetable dippers or baguette slices.

Nutritional Information

- Calories: 68
- Total Fat: 1g
- Saturated Fat: 0g
- Carbohydrates: 15g
- Protein: 2g

White Peppered Bean Dip

Ingredients

- 2 – 15 Ounce Cans of White Kidney Beans (Rinse and drained.)
- ½ Cup of Reduced Sodium Chicken Broth or Vegetable Broth
- 1 Tbsp. of Olive Oil
- 3 Minced Cloves of Garlic
- 1 tsp. of Fresh Marjoram – Snipped or ¼ tsp. of Dried Marjoram
- ½ tsp. of Fresh Rosemary – Snipped or 1/8 tsp. of Dried Crushed Rosemary
- 1/8 tsp. of Black Pepper
- Fresh Rosemary or Fresh Marjoram
- Whole Wheat Pita Chips
- 4 Whole Wheat Pita Bread (Rounds)
- 2 tsp. of Snipped Fresh Oregano
- Dash of Kosher Salt

Directions

1. In a 2-quart slow cooker, combine broth, beans, oil, marjoram, garlic, pepper, and rosemary.
2. Cover the beans and allow them to cook 3-4 hours.
3. Using a hand masher, mash the beans.
4. Spoon the mixture into a serving dish.
5. Sprinkle the fresh marjoram or the fresh rosemary on top.
6. Serve the dip warm or room temperature with pita chips.

5-Spice Tasty Chicken Wings

Ingredients

- **16-18 Chicken Wings (Approximately three pounds.)**
- **¾ Cup of Plum Sauce**
- **1 Tbsp. of Melted Butter**
- **1 tsp. of 5-Spice Powder**
- **Chopped Green Onions**

Directions

1. Preheat your oven to 375 degrees Fahrenheit.
2. Use a knife and cut the tips off the wings; carefully.
3. Cut the wings at the joints to make it into 2 pieces.
4. Line a 15x10x1 inch pan with aluminum foil.
5. Put the pieces in one layer and bake them for 20 minutes.
6. Drain the wings well.
7. In a 4 quart cooker, combine the butter, plum sauce, and the 5-spice powder.
8. Add the chicken and stir it in gently to coat all of the pieces with the sauce.
9. Cover the chicken and cook it on low heat for 3-4 hours or on high heat for 1 ½ - 2 hours.
10. Serve the chicken immediately or keep it warm in the cooker on low heat for up to an hour. Sprinkle the chopped green onions on top when you serve the tasty chicken.

Nutritional Information

- Calories: 32
- Total Fat: 1g
- Carbohydrates: 3g
- Protein: 3g

Hot Wing Dip

Ingredients

- **8 Ounces of Reduced Fat Cream Cheese or Neufchatel**
- **¼-1/2 Cup of Buffalo Sauce**
- **1 ½ Tbsp. of Reduced Calorie Blue Cheese Dressing**
- **1 Cup of Cooked Chicken Breast – Chopped**
- **1 Stalk of Finely Chipped Celery**
- **1 Seeded and Minced Jalapeno Pepper**
- **20 Halved Crosswise Celery Stalks**

Directions

1. In a 2-quart cooker, combine the wing sauce, cream cheese, chicken, dressing, chipped celery, and pepper.
2. Cover the mixture and cook it on low heat for 3-4 hours.
3. Serve it with the slices celery.

Nutritional Information

- Calories: 99
- Total Fat: 3g
- Saturated Fat: 3g
- Carbohydrates: 3g
- Protein: 7g

Italian Meatballs

Ingredients

- 1 – 12 Ounce Package of Cooked Turkey Meatballs (Thawed)
- ½ Cup of Roasted Red or Yellow Peppers (Cut into 1 inch pieces.)
- 1/8 tsp. of Crushed Red Pepper
- 1 Cup of Reduced Sodium Pasta Sauce
- Fresh Basil

Directions

1. Combine the roasted peppers and meatballs in a 2-quart slow cooker.
2. Sprinkle the crushed pepper on top.
3. Pour the sauce over the meatballs.
4. Cover the meatballs and cook them on low for 4-5 hours or on high for 2 hours.
5. Skim the fat from the sauce.
6. Stir the meatballs very gently before you serve them.
7. Serve them immediately or you can keep them warm on low for up to 2 hours.
8. Garnish the servings with the fresh basil.

Nutritional Information

- Calories: 68
- Total Fat: 1g
- Saturated Fat: 1g
- Carbohydrates: 3g
- Protein: 6g

Thai Peanut Sauce Chicken Wings

Ingredients

- **24 Chicken Wings (2 ¼ Pounds)**
- **¼ Cup of Water**
- **1 Tbsp. of Lime Juice**
- **¼ tsp. of Ground Ginger**
- **½ Cup of Creamy Peanut Butter**
- **½ Cup of Water**
- **2 Tbsp. of Reduced Sodium Soy Sauce**
- **2 Minced Cloves of Garlic**
- **½ tsp. of Ground Ginger**
- **¼ tsp. of Crushed Red Pepper**

Directions

1. Put the chicken in a 4-quart slow cooker.
2. Add ¼ cup of water, ¼ teaspoon of ginger, and lime juice.
3. Cover the chicken and cook it for 5-6 hours or on high for 2 ½ - 3 hours.
4. To prepare the peanut sauce, start by adding the peanut butter, soy sauce, remaining water, ginger, garlic, and the crushed red pepper in a small saucepan. Whisk everything together continuously.
5. Drain the chicken and toss the rest of the liquid.
6. Toss the chicken with half of the mixture.
7. You can place the chicken back into the slow cooker should you choose.
8. Serve the chicken with the rest of the sauce.

Nutritional Information

- Calories: 101
- Carbohydrates: 3g
- Protein: 9g

Spinach, Kale, and Artichoke Dip

Ingredients

- 3 Cloves of Crushed Garlic
- ½ Medium Onion
- 2 – 14 Ounces of Artichoke Hearts
- 10 Ounces of Chopped Spinach
- 10 Ounces of Chipped Kale
- 1 Cup of Parmesan Cheese
- 1 Cup of Shredded Skim Mozzarella
- 1 Cup of 0% Greek Yogurt
- ¾ Cup of Low Fat Sour Cream
- ¼ Cup of Low Fat Mayonnaise
- Dash of Salt
- Dash of Pepper

Directions

1. Using a food processor, add the artichokes, garlic, and onion into small pieces.
2. Add all the ingredients in the cooker and stir it together.
3. Cook the ingredients on high for four hours.

Nutritional Information

- Calories: 83
- Total Fat: 4.3g
- Saturated Fat: 0g
- Carbohydrates: 5.6g
- Protein: 6.5g

Chocolate Fondue Fruit Kabobs

Ingredients

- **1 – 8 Ounce of Light Whipped Topping (Thawed)**
- **16 – 6 Inch Skewers**
- **32 Halved Strawberries**
- **1 Pint of Raspberries**
- **32 Chunks of Pineapple**
- **¼ Cup of Strong Coffee (Hot)**

Directions

1. In a 2 quart cooker, combine chocolate pieces and whipped topping.
2. Cover the chocolate and allow it to cook on low for 30-45 minutes. Sir only 1 or 2 times.
3. Put the fruit on the skewers. (2 Raspberries, 2 Strawberries, 2 Pineapple Chunks)
4. Once the chocolate is completely melted, add the coffee and whisk it together (one tablespoon at a time).
5. To serve the fondue, keep it warm on the warm setting. You can add more coffee if it is too thick. Serve it with the kabobs.

Nutritional Information

- Calories: 159
- Total Fat: 5g
- Saturated Fat: 5g
- Carbohydrates: 21g
- Protein: 1g

Spicy Turkey Onion Bean Dip

Ingredients

- 4 Ounces of Uncooked Italian Sausage (Turkey)
- 1 – 15 Ounce Can of Reduced Fat Refined Beans
- ¾ Cup of Reduced Fat Monterey Jack Cheese – Shredded
- ¾ Cup of Salsa
- 2 Ounces of Un-drained Diced Green Chiles
- 2 Tbsp. of Reduced Fat Monterey Jack Cheese – Shredded
- 1 – 9 Ounce Bag of Scoop Tortilla Chips

Directions

1. In a medium pan, cook the sausage and the onion on medium, high heat. Make sure it is brown and breaks up.
2. Drain the fat from the meat.
3. Put the meat into a 2-quart cooker.
4. Stir in the beans, salsa, ¾ cup of cheese, and the chilies.
5. Cover the bean mixture and cook it on low for 3-4 hours.
6. Sir the beans very well before you serve it.
7. Sprinkle the remaining cheese on top and provide the chips.

Nutritional Information

- Calories: 76
- Total Fat: 1g
- Saturated Fat: 1g
- Carbohydrates: 12g
- Protein: 4g

Ingredients

- ¼ Cup of Butter
- ¼ Cup of Flour
- Dash of Salt
- ¼ tsp. of Ground Mustard
- ¼ tsp. of Pepper
- ¼ tsp. of Worcestershire Sauce
- 1 ½ Cups of Water
- 2 Cups of Cheddar Cheese – Shredded
- Ham Cubes, Bread Cubes, Sausage, or Broccoli Florets to Dip

Directions

1. In a medium saucepan, melt the butter.
2. Stir in the flour, the dash of salt, mustard, Worcestershire sauce, and pepper. Stir until it is smooth.
3. Gradually add the water.
4. Transfer the mixture into a 2-quart cooker.
5. Add the cheese and allow it to melt for 2 hours.
6. Serve the fondue with the sides of your choosing.

Nutritional Information

- Calories: 77
- Total Fat: 1g
- Saturated Fat: 1g
- Carbohydrates: 2g
- Protein: 3g

Maple Glazed Cocktail Sausages

Ingredients

- **16 Ounces of Cooked Polish Sausage or Smoke Turkey Sausages (Sliced into 1 inch slices)**
- **1/3 Cup of Apricot Preserves – Low Sugar**
- **3 Tbsp. Of Bourbon**
- **3 Tbsp. of Maple Syrup - Pure**
- **1 tsp. of Crushed Quick Cooking Tapioca**

Directions

1. In a 2 quart slow cooker add the apricot preserves, the sausage slices, bourbon, tapioca, and syrup.
2. Cover it and cook it on low for 4 hours.
3. Swerve is warm or immediately.

Nutritional Information

- Calories: 86
- Total Fat: 1g
- Saturated Fat: 1g
- Carbohydrates: 7g
- Protein: 8g

Pulled Barbecue Chicken

Ingredients

- **1 – 8 Ounce Can of Reduced Sodium Tomato Sauce**
- **1 – 4 Ounce Can of Drained Chopped Green Chiles**
- **3 Tbsp. of Cider Vinegar**
- **2 Tbsp. of Honey**
- **1 Tbsp. of Paprika**
- **1 Tbsp. of Worcestershire Sauce**
- **2 tsp. of Ground Chipotle Chile**
- **Dash of Salt**
- **2 ½ Pounds of Boneless Chicken Thighs**
- **1 Finely Chopped Small Onion**
- **1 Minced Clove of Garlic**

Directions

1. In a 6 quart slow cooker, put the chilies, vinegar, tomato sauce, honey, tomato paste, paprika, mustard, Worcestershire, salt, and ground chipotle and stir.
2. Add the chicken, garlic, and onion into the mixture.
3. Cover the chicken and cook it for 5 hours.
4. Transfer the chicken onto a cutting board and use a fork to shred it.
5. Put the chicken into the sauce and stir it thoroughly.
6. Serve it with bread or crackers.

Nutritional Information

- Calories: 364
- Total Fat: 13g
- Saturated Fat: 3g
- Carbohydrates: 32g
- Protein: 30 g

Irish Lamb and Potato Stew

Ingredients

- 2 Pounds of Boneless Lamb (Trimmed and cut into 1 inch pieces.)
- 1 ¾ Pounds of Potatoes (Peeled and cut into 1 inch cubes.)
- 3 Large White Parts of Leeks (Cut into 1 inch slices.)
- 3 Thinly Sliced Stalks of Celery
- 1 -14 Ounce can of Chicken Broth – Reduced Sodium
- 2 tsp. of Chopped Thyme
- Dash of Salt
- 1 tsp. of Pepper
- ¼ Cup of Chopped Parsley

Directions

1. Combine the potatoes, leeks, lamb, carrots, broth, celery, salt, thyme, and pepper in a 6-quart cooker and stir it thoroughly.
2. Allow it to cook covered for 8 hours.
3. Before you serve the stew, stir in the parsley.

Nutritional Information

- Calories: 76
- Total Fat: 1g
- Saturated Fat: 1g
- Carbohydrates: 12g
- Protein: 4g

Beef Hungarian Goulash

Ingredients

- 2 Pounds of Stew Meat (Cubed)
- 2 tsp. of Caraway Seeds
- 2 Tbsp. of Hungarian Paprika
- Dash of Salt and Pepper
- 2 Medium Chopped Onions
- 1 Small Chopped Red Bell Pepper
- 1 – 14 Ounce Can of Diced Tomatoes
- 1 – 14 Ounce Can of Beef Broth – Reduced Sodium
- 1 tsp. of Worcestershire Sauce
- 3 Minced Cloves of Garlic
- 2 Medium Sized Bay Leaves
- 1 Tbsp. of Cornstarch (Mix with 2 Tbsp. of water.)
- 2 Tbsp. of Chopped Parsley

Directions

1. Put the beef in a 4-quart cooker.
2. Crush the caraway seeds and put in a small mixing bowl with the paprika, pepper, and salt.
3. Sprinkle the mixtures onto the beef and coat it well.
4. Add the onion and the bell pepper.
5. In a medium pan, add the tomatoes, Worcestershire sauce, broth, and garlic and allow it to come to a simmer.
6. Pour the mixture over the vegetable and the beef.
7. Put the bay leaves on top of the beef.
8. Cover the beef and cook it on high for 5 hours or on low for 8 hours.
9. Remove the bay leaves and skim off the visible fat.

10. Add the cornstarch to the stew and cook it on high for 10-15 minutes, then sprinkle the parsley on top.

Nutritional Information

- Calories: 177
- Total Fat: 5g
- Saturated Fat: 2g
- Carbohydrates: 7g
- Protein: 25g

Cornbread Crockpot Chicken Dressing

Ingredients

- **Cornbread**
- **3 Boneless Boiled Chicken Breasts**
- **Dash of Sage**
- **2 Cans of Chicken Stock**
- **Dash of Salt and Pepper**
- **1 Medium Chopped Onion**

Directions

1. Crumble the cornbread into a 4-quart slow cooker.
2. Shred the chicken and mix it into the cornbread gently.
3. Add the pepper, salt, onion, and the sage into the mixture and stir it gently.
4. Cook it for 1-½ hours.
5. Serve it hot.

Nutritional Information

- Calories: 295
- Total Fat: 6g
- Saturated Fat: 1g
- Carbohydrates: 43g
- Protein: 12g

Italian Cream Cheese Chicken

Ingredients

- **1 Can of Cream of Chicken Soup**
- **8 Ounces of Water**
- **1 – 8 Ounce of Cream Cheese – Low Fat**
- **1 Package of Italian Dry Mix Dressing**
- **1 – 2 Pounds of Boneless Chicken Breasts**
- **Rice or Noodles**

Directions

1. In a 4 quart slow cooker, mix in the water, soup, and the dry dressing spices.
2. Place the cream cheese and the chicken into the cooker.
3. Cover the mixture and cook it on low for 7 hours of on high for 4 hours.
4. Remove the chicken and shred it with a fork.
5. Put the chicken back into the cooker and set the cooker to warm.
6. Cook the noodles or rice.
7. Pour the chicken over the noodles or rice and serve it.

Nutritional Information

- Calories: 197.2
- Total Fat: 5.3g
- Saturated Fat: 5.3g
- Carbohydrates: 14.4g
- Protein: 9.5g

Ingredients

Marinade:

- **2.5 Pounds of Lean Pork Tenderloin**
- **1 Tbsp. of Dijon Mustard**
- **2 tsp. of Ground ginger**
- **2 tsp. of Curry Powder**
- **2 tsp. of Ground Coriander**
- **½ tsp. of Pepper**
- **½ Tbsp. of Rice Wine Vinegar**

Glaze:

- **2 Tbsp. of Honey**
- **1 tsp. of Garlic Powder**
- **1 tsp. of Onion Powder**
- **2 Tbsp. of Soy Sauce – Lite**
- **2 Tbsp. of Rice Wine Vinegar**
- **1 Tbsp. of Water – Warm**
- **1 tsp. of Sesame Oil**
- **1 Tbsp. of Dijon Mustard**

Directions

1. In a large bowl, mix all of the marinade ingredients.
2. Trim the tenderloin and cut it into 1-inch squares.
3. Put the tenderloin pieces in the marinade.
4. Allow the meat to marinate over night.
5. Put the meat in a 4-quart cooker on low for 6-8 hours or on high for 3-4 hours.
6. In a medium saucepan, add all the glaze ingredients and cook it on medium heat for four minutes. Stir it constantly.

7. Put the meat on a serving dish and pour the glaze on the meat. Stir the meat lightly.

Nutritional Information

- Calories: 178
- Total Fat: 4g
- Saturated Fat: 1g
- Carbohydrates: 8g
- Protein: 25g

Cheddar and Broccoli Soup

Ingredients

- ¼ Cup of Whole Wheat Flour
- 2 Tbsp. of Extra Virgin Olive Oil
- 4 Cups of Chicken Broth – Low Fat and Low Sodium
- 1 Pounds of Frozen Broccoli – Thawed
- 2 tsp. of Garlic Powder
- Dash of Salt and Pepper
- Cooking Spray

Directions

1. In a medium pan, add oil over medium low heat and do not allow it to boil.
2. Slowly whisk in the flour a small bit at a time.
3. Slowly whisk in the broth.
4. Spray the cooker with cooking spray.
5. Pour the mixture into a 4-quart cooker.
6. Add the broccoli into the cooker and allow it to cook for 4-6 hours.
7. Add the cheese and mix it thoroughly.
8. When the cheese is melted, add the salt and pepper.
9. Add the garlic powder and serve.

Nutritional Information

- Calories: 168
- Total Fat: 13g
- Saturated Fat: 7g
- Carbohydrates: 4g
- Protein: 10g

Ingredients

- **1 Tbsp. of Extra Virgin Olive Oil**
- **1 Diced Stalk of Celery**
- **½ Cup of Diced Onion**
- **1 Minced Clove of Garlic**
- **3 Cups of Cubed Turkey**
- **1 Cup of Diced (1 inch) Sweet Potatoes**
- **2 Cups of Sliced Carrots**
- **½ tsp. of Pepper**
- **1/8 tsp. of All Spice**
- **1 Whole Bay Leaf**
- **1 tsp. of Red Pepper**
- **½ tsp. of Cayenne Pepper**

Directions

1. Sauté the celery, garlic, and onion in the olive oil.
2. Add the onion mixture to a 4-quart slow cooker.
3. Add the rest of the ingredients to the cooker.
4. Cook the stew for 8 hours.

Nutritional Information

- Calories: 183
- Total Fat: 4g
- Saturated Fat: 0g
- Carbohydrates: 7g
- Protein: 21g

Cooker Pot Roast

Ingredients

- **2 ½ Pounds of Rump Roast**
- **2 Tbsp. of Cornstarch**
- **2 Tbsp. of Dry Tapioca**
- **10 Minced Cloves of Garlic**
- **3 Large Carrots – Sliced**
- **1 Pound of Small Red Potatoes – Peeled**
- **2 Cups of Beef Broth – Lite**
- **1 Tbsp. of Balsamic Vinegar**
- **2 Tbsp. of Onion Flakes**
- **Dash of Pepper**
- **Dash of Salt**

Directions

1. Spray your 5-quart cooker with cooking spray.
2. Pour in the broth.
3. Mix in the tapioca and cornstarch.
4. Stir in the dry ingredients, garlic, and vinegar.
5. Add the beef and turn over once.
6. Add in the vegetables and allow it to cook for 8 hours on low or for 4 hours on high.

Nutritional Information

- Calories: 316
- Total Fat: 11.4g
- Saturated Fat: 4.4g
- Carbohydrates: 4g
- Protein: 34g

Slow Cooker Short Ribs

Ingredients

- ¾ **Cup of Soy Sauce – Low Sodium**
- ¼ **Cup of Splenda Brown Sugar**
- ¾ **Cup of Water**
- **2 Pounds of Short Ribs – Beef of Pork**

Directions

1. Put all of the ingredients in a 5-quart cooker.
2. Cook the ribs on low for 8 hours if the ribs are frozen.
3. Cook the ribs on high for 1 hour on high if the meat is thawed.

Nutritional Information

- Calories: 310
- Total Fat: 15g
- Saturated Fat: 0g
- Carbohydrates: 15g
- Protein: 29g

Slow Cooker Harvest Potatoes and Chicken

Ingredients

- 1 Pounds of Boneless Chicken Breast – Cubed into 1 inch.
- 3 Tbsp. of Flour
- Dash of Salt
- Dash of Pepper
- 12 Ounces of New Potatoes – Halved
- 2 Cups of Baby Carrots – Cut into 3 pieces.
- 2 Stalks of Celery Cut in ½
- 1 Large Chopped Onion
- 1 Can of Sliced and Drained Mushrooms
- 2 Minced Cloves of Garlic
- ¾ tsp. of Dried Thyme
- ¼ tsp. Of Sage
- 1 Cup of Chicken Broth – Low Sodium
- 1 Tbsp. of Butter

Directions

1. In a medium-mixing bowl, add 2 tablespoons of flour, chicken, salt, and pepper.
2. Add the chicken mixture to a 4-quart slow cooker.
3. Stir in the carrots, onions, celery, potatoes, garlic, mushrooms, ½ teaspoon of thyme, broth, and sage.
4. Cover the chicken and cook it on high for 4 hours or on low for 6-7 hours.
5. In a small mixing bowl, add the remaining flour, melted butter, and mix it thoroughly.
6. Add in the salt, thyme, and flour. Mix it until it is thick.
7. Add it to the chicken and allow it to cook for 1 more hour.

Shredded Beef Stew

Ingredients

- 1 ½ Cups of Chicken Broth – Reduced Sodium
- ¼ Cup of Sherry Vinegar
- 2 Stalks of Sliced Celery
- 1 Large Chopped Onion
- 1 Large Chopped Red Bell Pepper
- 3 Mined Cloves Garlic
- 1 Tbsp. of Ground Cumin
- Dash of Salt
- Dash of Pepper
- 3 Pounds of Flank Steak
- ½ Cup of Cilantro Leaves – Chopped
- ½ Cup of Pickled Jalapenos – Chopped
- 10 Heated Corn Tortillas

Directions

1. Combine the vinegar, broth, and onion, celery, bell pepper, cumin, garlic, salt, and pepper in a 6-quart cooker.
2. Add in the beef ensuring it is submerge and put the vegetables underneath.
3. Put the id on the cooker and allow it to cook for 8 hours on low.
4. Transfer the steak onto a cutting board and allow it to stand for 10 minutes.
5. Shred the steak with a fork and put it back into the cooker.
6. Stir in the cilantro and garnish with the jalapeno.
7. Serve it with the warm tortillas.

Nutritional Information

- Calories: 224

Chicken Noodle Soup

Ingredients

- 1 – 3 Pounds of Boneless Chicken Breasts
- 2 Peeled and Quartered Large Onions
- 3 Peeled and Quartered Large Carrots
- 2 Diced Carrots
- ½ tsp. of Crushed Thyme
- ½ tsp. of Crushed Marjoram
- ¼ tsp. of Pepper
- 1 Quart Chicken Broth – No Salt No Fat
- 1 Quart of Boiling Water
- 6 Ounce of Medium Wide Egg Noodles - Cooked
- 4 Ounces of Sliced Mushrooms
- ½ Pound of Spinach
- 2 Diced Celery Stalks

Directions

1. Put the chicken in a 5 quart cooker.
2. Add in the onion, carrots, and parsley.
3. Sprinkle the vegetables and chicken with the pepper, thyme, and marjoram.
4. Add the chicken broth and cook it for 7-8 hours on low or 3 hours on low.
5. Remove the chicken and shred it with the forks.
6. Add the chicken back into the cooker.
7. Allow it to simmer for 10 minutes.
8. Before you serve the soup, add in some cooked noodles and pepper.

Swiss Steak Made Easy

Ingredients

- 1 ½ Pounds of Beef Round Steak – Sliced
- ½ tsp. of Thyme
- ¼ tsp. of Paprika
- 1 Tbsp. of Worcestershire Sauce
- Cooking Spray
- 1 Sliced Clove of Garlic
- 2 Celery Ribs Sliced
- 2 Medium Thinly Sliced Onions
- 4 Medium Tomatoes Sliced Thin
- ½ Cup of Beef Broth – Reduced Sodium

Directions

1. Combine the thyme, paprika, thyme.
2. Brush the steak with the Worcestershire sauce.
3. Dredge the steak in the flour mixture.
4. Spray a large pan with cooking spray.
5. On medium high heat, put the steak pieces in the pan and brown both sides for 5 minutes.
6. Place the steak in a 3-quart cooker.
7. Top it with garlic, onions, tomatoes, and celery.
8. Pour the beef broth on top. (Do not stir.)
9. Cook the steak for 8-9 hours on low or 4-5 hours on high.
10. In order to serve the steak, remove the steak and vegetables from the booker and put it in a serving dish.
11. Spoon the left over liquid on top of the serving dish.

Slow Cooker Steak Tacos

Ingredients

- **1 Pounds of Flank Steak – Semi Frozen**
- **1 Packet of Taco Seasoning**
- **1 Chopped Medium Onion**
- **4 Ounce of Green Chilies – Chopped**
- **½ Cup of Sliced Bell Peppers**
- **1 Package of Tortillas**

Directions

1. Cut the steaks in half.
2. Rub the taco seasoning on the meat.
3. Place the meat into a 2-quart slow cooker.
4. Top it with onion, chilies, and bell pepper.
5. Cover the meat and cook it on low for 8-9 hours.
6. Remove the steak and allow it to sit for approximately 5 minutes.
7. Shred the steak with forks.
8. Return the meat to the crock-pot.
9. Spoon ½ cup of the mixture in the middle of each tortilla.
10. Top them with cheese, sour cream, and tomato.

Nutritional Information

- Calories: 152
- Total Fat: 8g
- Saturated Fat: 1g
- Carbohydrates: 4g
- Protein: 15g

Slow Cooker Cheeseburgers

Ingredients

- 1 ½ Pounds of Ground Beef
- ¼ tsp. of Garlic Salt
- ½ tsp. of Pepper
- 2 Tbsp. of Water
- 1 Cup of Onion – Chopped
- 2 Minced Cloves of Garlic
- 1 Tbsp. of Prepared Mustard
- 1 Tbsp. of Dill Relish
- 8 Ounces of Light Velveeta Cheese

Directions

1. Brown the beef in a large pan until it is completely brown.
2. Spray the cooker with cooking spray and put the beef in.
3. Stir in the pepper, water, garlic salt, onion, mustard, garlic, cheese, and relish.
4. Cover the mixture and allow it to cook for 2-3 hours.
5. Stir the beef and serve it on bread or buns.

Nutritional Information

- Calories: 181
- Total Fat: 7g
- Saturated Fat: 1g
- Carbohydrates: 7g
- Protein: 21g

Slow Cooker Japanese Lamb

Ingredients

- **2 Pounds of Lamb**
- **¼ Cup of Soy Sauce – Reduced Sodium**
- **1 Tbsp. of Honey**
- **2 Tbsp. of Vinegar**
- **2 Tbsp. of Sherry**
- **2 Crushed Garlic Cloves**
- **¼ tsp. of Ground Ginger**
- **1 ½ Cup of Chicken Stock**

Directions

1. Put all the ingredients in a slow cooker for 10 hours on low.
2. Put the lamb in a serving dish and pour the left over liquid on top.

Nutritional Information

- Calories: 257
- Total Fat: 19g
- Saturated Fat: 1g
- Carbohydrates: 4g
- Protein: 15g

Ingredients

- **12 Chicken Thighs or Legs**
- **1 Jar of No-Sugar-Added Marinara Sauce**
- **¼ Cup of Onion Flakes**
- **Dash of Salt**
- **½ tsp. of Garlic Powder**
- **½ tsp. of Red Pepper**

Directions

1. Clean the chicken and discard the chicken skin.
2. Put the pieces into the cooker.
3. Add the onion, salt, sauce, garlic, and red pepper.

Nutritional Information

- Calories: 661
- Total Fat: 41g
- Saturated Fat: 1g
- Carbohydrates: 6g
- Protein: 62g

Corned Beef and Cabbage

Ingredients

- **4 Cups of Hot Water**
- **2 Tbsp. of Cider Vinegar**
- **2 Tbsp. of Splenda**
- **½ tsp. of Pepper**
- **1 Large Wedged Onion**
- **3 Pounds of Corned Beef**
- **1 Full Cabbage – Cored**

Directions

1. Cut the cabbage into 10 wedges.
2. In a 6 quart slow cooker add in the water, vinegar, pepper, Splenda, onions, and mix it well.
3. Put the corned beef into the mix.
4. Cover it and cook it for 4 hours on low.
5. Remove the lid and put the cabbage wedges over the top of the corned beef.
6. Cover the corned beef and cook for an additional 3-4 hours.
7. Serve the beef in slices with cabbage and a spoon full of the liquid to keep the meat moist.

Nutritional Information

- Calories: 436
- Total Fat: 33g
- Saturated Fat: 1g
- Carbohydrates: 2g
- Protein: 31g

Shredded Beef Slow Cooker Sandwiches

Ingredients

- **3 Pounds of Boneless Roast – Beef**
- **1 Chopped Medium Onion**
- **1/3 Cup of Vinegar**
- **3 Whole Bay Leaves**
- **Dash of Salt**
- **¼ tsp. of Ground Cloves**
- **1/8 tsp. of Garlic Powder**
- **12 Split Hamburger Buns**

Directions

1. Cut the roast in two pieces.
2. Put it in the slow cooker and add the onion, bay leaves, garlic powder, vinegar, salt, and cloves.
3. Allow it to cook for 10-12 hours.
4. Remove the bay leaves and shred the meat with forks.
5. Serve on the buns.

Nutritional Information

- Calories: 173
- Total Fat: 6g
- Saturated Fat: 1g
- Carbohydrates: 2g
- Protein: 26g

Spicy and Juicy Beef Roast

Ingredients

- **4 Pounds of Boneless Chuck Roast**
- **Dash of Salt and Pepper**
- **2 Tbsp. of Cooking Oil**
- **½ Cup of Water**
- **1 Tbsp. of Worcestershire Sauce**
- **1 Tbsp. of Tomato Paste**
- **2 Minced Cloves of Garlic**
- **10 Dashes of Hot Sauce**
- **1 Tbsp. of Cornstarch**
- **1 Tbsp. of Cold Water**
- **1 Tbsp. of Horseradish**

Directions

1. Trim the fat off of the meat.
2. Put the meat in a 5-quart slow cooker.
3. Sprinkle the roast with pepper and salt.
4. In a small mixing bowl add ½ cup of water, tomato paste, Worcestershire sauce, garlic, and hot sauce.
5. Pour the mixture over the meat.
6. Cook the meat for 10-12 hours on low or 5-6 hours on high.
7. Strain the cooking liquid and skim all of the fat possible.
8. Transfer the liquid to a medium pan.
9. In a small mixing bowl add the water, corn starch and stir it into the pan.
10. Cook and whisk it over medium heat until it is thick and produces bubbles.
11. Cook it for 2 more minutes.

12. Stir in the horseradish and the ½ teaspoon of salt.

13. Serve the mixture over the meat.

Nutritional Information

- Calories: 203
- Total Fat: 6g
- Saturated Fat: 1g
- Carbohydrates: 2g
- Protein: 34g

Comfort Chili

Ingredients

- 1 Pounds of Turkey Breast or Ground Beef
- 1 Finely Chopped Medium Onion
- 5 Ounce of Pinto Beans – Drained and rinsed.
- 8 ½ Ounces of Corn – Drained and rinsed.
- 15 Ounce of Tomato Sauce
- 14 ½ Ounce of Diced Tomatoes
- 10 Ounce of Diced Green Chilies and Tomatoes
- 1 Tbsp. of Chili Powder
- 1 tsp. of Ground Cumin
- ½ tsp. of Garlic Powder
- Dash of Salt

Directions

1. In a medium sized pan add the ground meat and brown it thoroughly.
2. Drain the meat and add it to a 4 quart cooker.
3. Add all the other ingredients and cook it for 4 hours on high.
4. Stir the chili after 2 hours of cooking.

Nutritional Information

- Calories: 76
- Total Fat: 1g
- Saturated Fat: 1g
- Carbohydrates: 12g
- Protein: 4g

Dried Tomatoes and Beans

Ingredients

- 3 Cans of White Kidney Beans
- 1 Can of Vegetable Broth
- 3 Minced Garlic Cloves
- 7 Ounces of Sun Dried and Oil packed Tomatoes – Chopped and Drained
- 2 Ounces of Shaved Asiago Cheese
- 1/3 Cup of Pine Nuts

Directions

1. In a 4-quart cooker combine vegetables, beans, broth, and garlic.
2. Cover the mixture and cook it on low for 6-8 hours or on high for 4 hours.
3. Stir in tomatoes, if you have it on the low setting turn it to high when you add the tomatoes.
4. Cover it and cook it for 15 more minutes.
5. Serve it with the cheese sprinkled on top.

Nutritional Information

- Calories: 242
- Total Fat: 9g
- Saturated Fat: 3g
- Carbohydrates: 1g
- Protein: 16g

Ingredients

- **2 Pounds of Boneless Chicken Breast**
- **1 Can of Red Enchilada Sauce**
- **1 Can of Diced Green Chilies**
- **¾ Cup of Diced Onion**
- **Whole Wheat Flour Tortillas**
- **Shredded Cheddar Cheese**
- **Tomatoes – Diced**
- **Shredded Lettuce**
- **Sour Cream**
- **Salsa**

Directions

1. Put the chicken, green chilies, enchilada sauce, and onion in the 4-quart cooker.
2. Shred the chicken with forks.
3. Serve on the tortilla and add lettuce, sour cream, cheese, and tomatoes.

Nutritional Information

- Calories: 210
- Total Fat: 9.5g
- Saturated Fat: 2g
- Carbohydrates: 14g
- Protein: 19g

Slow Cooker Chicken Creole

Ingredients

- **4 Boneless Chicken Breasts**
- **Dash of Salt and Pepper**
- **Creole Seasoning**
- **1 – 14.5 Ounces of Stewed Tomatoes**
- **1 Diced Celery Stalk**
- **1 Diced Green Bell Pepper**
- **3 Minced Cloves of Garlic**
- **1 Diced Onion**
- **1 – 4 Ounce of Drained Mushrooms**
- **1 Jalapeno Pepper – Chopped**

Directions

1. Put the chicken breasts in the cooker.
2. Season with pepper, salt, and the Creole seasoning.
3. Stir in the tomatoes with the liquid, bell pepper, celery, garlic, onion, jalapeno pepper, and mushrooms.
4. Cook it on low for 10-12 hours or 5-6 hours on high.

Nutritional Information

- Calories: 191
- Total Fat: 1.8g
- Saturated Fat: 1g
- Carbohydrates: 14.3g
- Protein: 29.6g

Ingredients

- 1 Can of Drained and Pitted Plumes
- ½ Cup of Orange Juice
- ¼ Cup of Chopped Onion
- 1 Tbsp. of Fresh Ginger
- ¼ tsp. of Cinnamon
- 1 Pound of Boneless Turkey Breast – Cut into strips.
- 6 – 7 inch Flour Tortillas
- 3 Cups of Coleslaw Mix

Directions

1. Put the plums in a food processor and blend them until they are smooth.
2. Combine the orange juice, plums, onion, cinnamon, and ginger into a 4-quart cooker.
3. Put the turkey on the plum mixture and cook it for 3-4 hours.
4. Remove the turkey and put it in the tortillas.
5. Spoon 2 tablespoons of the plum sauce on the turkey.
6. Top it with ½ cup of coleslaw mix.

Nutritional Information

- Calories: 248
- Total Fat: 4g
- Saturated Fat: 1g
- Carbohydrates: 36g
- Protein: 17g

Peek A Boo Chicken Casserole

Ingredients

- **2 Pounds of Boneless Chicken Breasts – Cubed**
- **1 Package of Onion Soup Mix**
- **1 Can of Beef Broth – Fat Free**
- **1 Can of Cream of Mushroom Soup – 98% Fat Free**
- **4 Ounces of Drained Mushrooms**

Directions

1. Put all ingredients into a 3-quart slow cooker.
2. Cover and cook the chicken for 8-10 hours on low or 3-4 hours on high.
3. Serve it on rice or noodles.

Nutritional Information

- Calories: 291
- Total Fat: 4g
- Saturated Fat: 0g
- Carbohydrates: 3g
- Protein: 57g

Dude Ranch Steak Soup

Ingredients

- 2 Pounds of Round Steak – Cut into bite size.
- 1 – 15.5 Ounce Can of Drained Kidney Beans
- 1 – 4 Ounce Can of Green Chilies – Chopped
- 3 Finely Chopped Celery Stalks
- 1 – 14.5 Ounce Can of Beef Broth
- 1 Tbsp. of Tomato Paste
- 1 tsp. of Chili Powder
- 1 tsp. of Adobo Seasoning
- 1 Cube of Beef Bouillon
- 1 tsp. of Pepper
- 1 tsp. of Cumin
- 1 tsp. of Minced Garlic
- 3 Tbsp. of Dried Minced Onions
- 1 Cup of Shredded Cheddar Cheese – Reduced Fat

Directions

1. Add all of the ingredients (except for the cheddar cheese) into 4-quart slow cooker.
2. Cook it for 7.5 hours on low.
3. Stir in the cheese and cook for another 30 minutes.

Nutritional Information

- Calories: 398
- Total Fat: 11g
- Saturated Fat: 1g
- Carbohydrates: 11.5g
- Protein: 53g

Artichoke and Rosemary Chicken

Ingredients

- 1 Chopped Medium Onion
- 6 Minced Cloves of Garlic
- 1/3 Cups of Chicken Broth – Reduced Sodium
- 1 Tbsp. of Quick Cooking Tapioca
- 2 tsp. of Finely Shredded Lemon Peel
- 2 tsp. of Died Rosemary
- ¾ tsp. of Pepper
- 2 ½ Pounds of Skinned Chicken Thighs
- Dash of Salt
- 8 Ounces of Artichoke Hearts
- 1 Chopped Medium Red Bell Pepper

Directions

1. In a 4-quart cooker, combine the garlic, broth, onion, tapioca, 1-teaspoon lemon peel, rosemary, and a dash of pepper.
2. Cover the chicken and allow it to cook for 5 hours on high or 3 hours on low.
3. Add the artichoke hearts and peppers.
4. Cook for another 30 minutes.
5. Sprinkle the remaining lemon on top when it is served.

Nutritional Information

- Calories: 168
- Total Fat: 4g
- Saturated Fat: 1g
- Carbohydrates: 8g
- Protein: 23g

Garden Bounty Style Tomato Soup

Ingredients

- **2 Pounds of Chopped Roma Tomatoes**
- **2 – 14 Ounce Cans of Beef Broth**
- **2 Cups of Finely Chopped Vegetables – Celery, Sweet Pepper, Carrot, Onions)**
- **1 – 6 Ounce Can of Tomato Paste**
- **1 tsp. of Sugar**

Directions

1. In a 4-quart cooker combine beef broth, tomatoes, vegetables, sugar, and tomato paste.
2. Cover it and cook on low for 6-8 hours or on high for 3-4 hours.

Nutritional Information

- Calories: 56
- Total Fat: 0g
- Saturated Fat: 0g
- Carbohydrates: 11g
- Protein: 3g

Vegetable Curry

Ingredients

- **3 Chopped Potatoes**
- **1 Chopped Cauliflower**
- **1 ½ Cups of Green Peas**
- **3 Chopped Tomatoes**
- **¾ tsp. of Turmeric**
- **½ tsp. of Chili Powder**
- **1 ½ tsp. of Cumin**
- **1 tsp. of Curry**
- **1 Cup of Water**

Directions

1. Place all of the ingredients in a 3-quart slow cooker.
2. Cook it on low for 5-6 hours.

Nutritional Information

- Calories: 125
- Total Fat: 0g
- Saturated Fat: 0g
- Carbohydrates: 26.5g
- Protein: 5g

Cranberry Pork Chops

Ingredients

- **6 Bone-In Pork Chops**
- **1 – 16 Ounce can of Cranberry Sauce**
- **½ Cup of Apple Juice**
- **¼ Cup of Sugar**
- **2 Tbsp. of Spicy Brown Mustard**
- **2 Tbsp. of Cornstarch**
- **¼ Cup of Cold Water**
- **Dash of Salt**
- **Dash of Pepper**

Directions

1. Put the pork chops in the cooker.
2. Combine the juice, cranberry sauce, mustard, and the sugar.
3. Pour it over the pork.
4. Cook on low for 7-8 hours.
5. In a medium sized pan add the cornstarch and cold water. Mix until it is completely smooth.
6. Stir in the cooking juices and bring it to a boil.
7. Stir in the pepper and salt.
8. Serve it over the pork.

Nutritional Information

- Calories: 397
- Total Fat: 9g
- Saturated Fat: 3g
- Carbohydrates: 42g
- Protein: 24g

Salmon Patties

Ingredients

- **2 Fork Beaten Large Eggs**
- **2.75 Ounce of Drained Salmon**
- **½ Cup of Water**
- **1 Cup of Soda Cracker Crumbs**
- **½ tsp. of Celery Salt**
- **¼ tsp. of Dried Dill Weed**
- **Dash of Pepper**
- **½ Cup of Cornflake Crumbs**

Directions

1. Mix all of the ingredients (except for the cornflakes) in a large mixing bowl.
2. Shape the salmon into patties.
3. Coat the patties with the cornflakes.
4. Put the patties in the bottom of a 5-quart cooker.
5. Put the remaining patties on top.
6. Cook them for 4-5 hours on low or 2-2 ½ hours on high.

Nutritional Information

- Calories: 171
- Total Fat: 8g
- Saturated Fat: 0g
- Carbohydrates: 13g
- Protein: 11g

Lemon Dill Slow Cooker Chicken

Ingredients

- **1 Cup of Sour Cream – Fat Free**
- **1 Tbsp. Minced Dill**
- **1 tsp. of Lemon Pepper**
- **1 tsp. of Lemon Zest**
- **4 Boneless Chicken breasts – Halves**

Directions

1. Combine the dill, sour cream, lemon pepper, and lemon zest.
2. Spoon some of the mixture onto the bottom of the cooker.
3. Put the chicken in one layer on top of the sour cream mixture.
4. Pour the remaining sauce onto the chicken evenly.
5. Cook it on low for 3-4 hours.

Nutritional Information

- Calories: 170
- Total Fat: 0g
- Saturated Fat: 0g
- Carbohydrates: 7g
- Protein: 26g

Tex Mex Lime Flavored Pork and Onions

Ingredients

- 1 – 14 Ounce Jar of Roasted Ranchero Cooking sauce
- 1 – 4 Ounce Can of Diced Green Chilies
- 3 ½ Pounds of Bone In Pork Shoulder Roast
- 1 Medium Sliced Red Onion
- ¼ Cup of Lime Juice
- ½ Cup of Chopped Cilantro
- Warm Corn Tortillas

Directions

1. In a medium-mixing bowl, combine the sauce and chilies.
2. Place the pork into a 4-quart cooker and spoon the sauce over it.
3. Cover the pork and cook it for 8-10 hours.
4. Twenty minutes before it is served, add the onion slices with the lime ice in a medium mixing bowl and toss it three times.
5. Remove the pork to the cutting board.
6. Stir the cilantro into the mixture.
7. Break the pork into bite sized pieces with a wooden spoon.
8. Put the pork back into the cooker and stir it.
9. Spoon the pork over warm tortillas. Top with marinated onions.

Nutritional Information

- Calories: 268
- Total Fat: 12g
- Saturated Fat: 4g
- Carbohydrates: 9g
- Protein: 29g

Chicken Enchilada Stack

Ingredients:

- 1 teaspoon canola oil
- 1 cup onion; chopped
- ½ cup poblano, seeded and chopped
- 2 minced cloves garlic
- 1 ½ teaspoon chipotle chili powder
- 1 14.5 oz. diced tomatoes; drained and no salt added
- 1 8 oz. canned tomato sauce; Italian seasoned
- Cooking spray
- 2 cups rotisserie chicken breast; shredded
- 1 cup frozen; white and yellow corn
- 1 15 oz. can black beans; drained and rinsed
- 5 corn and flour tortillas
- 8 oz. shredded cheddar cheese; reduced fat
- Cilantro sprigs

Method:

1.   1.Using a nonstick skillet heat on medium and add oil. Add onion, pepper, and garlic; cook until tender; about 6 minutes.

2.   Stir in chili powder, tomatoes, and tomato sauce. Put half the tomato mixture in a blender. Remove lid of blender and let steam escape. Place a towel over blender and blend until almost smooth and pour into a bowl. Repeat process with the other half of tomato mixture.

3. Spray slow cooker with non stick cooking spray. Spread 3 tablespoons of tomato mixture on bottom of slow cooker. Mix the remainder of tomato mixture with chicken, corn, and beans.

4. Place one tortilla on the tomato mixture in slow cooker. Cover with 1 cup of chicken mixture. Sprinkle with cheese; about 1/3 cup. Top with another tortilla and repeat process until all tortillas and chicken mixture are in slow cooker.

5. Cook on low setting for 2 hours or until the cheese is melted and the edges are browned.

Nutritional Information:

Calories; 295, Fats 10.3g, Carbohydrates 16g, Protein 24g

Thank You!

Recipe Junkies Alert!

Sign up for Recipe Junkies FREE Newsletter today and never pay more than a buck for a brand new recipe book! Receive alerts about new recipe books before they even come out! We have many other awesome offers for subscribers eyes only! You can follow us on Facebook and Twitter as well!

Come he a part of the Recipe Junkies family where recipes are our business and business is good! You are more than just a number to us and we appreciate all of our newsletter subscribers. Email us for more info at recipejunkies1@gmail.com

Recipe Junkies Alert Promo
Recipe Junkies Facebook
Recipe Junkies Twitter

Check out other Amazon best sellers from the Recipe Junkie family!

Made in the USA
Lexington, KY
25 June 2015